General Elections today

Second edition

Frank Conley

Manchester University Press

Manchester and New York

Distributed exclusively in the USA and Canada by St. Martin's Press

Published by Manchester University Press
Oxford Road, Manchester M13 9NR, UK
and Room 400, 175 Fifth Avenue, New York, NY 10010, USA

Distributed exclusively in the USA and Canada
by St. Martin's Press, Inc., 175 Fifth Avenue, New York,
NY 10010, USA

British Library Cataloguing-in-Publication Data
A catalogue record for this book is available from the British Library

Library of Congress Cataloging-in-Publication Data
Conley, Frank, 1946–
　　　General elections today/Frank Conley. — 2nd ed.
　　　　　p.　　cm.—(Politics today)
　　　Includes bibliographical references (p.) and index.
　　　ISBN 0–7190–3952–5 (hardback).—ISBN 0–7190–3953–3 (paperback)
　　　1. Elections—Great Britain. 2. Great Britain—Politics and
government—1945– I. Title. II. Series: Politics today
(Manchester, England)
JN956.066　1994
324.941085—dc20　　　93–50582

ISBN 0 7190 3952 5 *hardback*
0 7190 3953 3 *paperback*

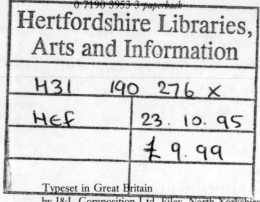
Typeset in Great Britain
by J&L Composition Ltd, Filey, North Yorkshire
Printed in Great Britain
by Bell & Bain Ltd, Glasgow

Contents

List of figures and tables

Figures

Tables

List of abbreviations

AUEW	Amalgamated Union of Engineering Workers
CBI	Confederation of British Industry
CND	Campaign for Nuclear Disarmament
ERM	Exchange Rate Mechanism
GLC	Greater London Council
MEP	Member of European Parliament
NEC	National Executive Committee
NUM	National Union of Mineworkers
NUPE	National Union of Public Employees
PR	Proportional Representation
SDP	Social Democratic Party
SNP	Scottish National Party
TGWU	Transport and General Workers Union
TUC	Trades Union Congress
VAT	Value Added Tax

Preface and acknowledgements

The General Election of 1992 has provided the opportunity for a substantial revision of *General Elections Today*. As well as the chapter on 1992, the General Elections of 1964 and 1966 now have separate chapters, and the elections 1945–1959 are discussed at greater length. This expansion of the historical context should not only help politics students whose historical understanding begins with Mrs Thatcher, but should make the book even more useful in courses in twentieth century history, since it covers many of the most important political developments of the last half-century. The central chapters on the elections 1970–1987 are untouched, but all the other chapters have been largely re-written to take account of recent research and writing as well as the longer perspective of the period 1945–1992: in addition a final chapter deals with the topic of electoral and constitutional reform, which came on to the political agenda in 1992 to an extent not seen in immediately preceding elections. Many of the figures and tables have been revised and extended.

I am very grateful to several groups of people who have helped in bringing this book to fruition. Manchester University Press, and Richard Purslow in particular, have shown confidence in asking me to revise and expand it, and to include visual material. I am very grateful to a number of individuals and organisations who have given permission for me to use copyright material: they are listed below. I have tried to respond to all those, reviewers and friends, who have made positive comments about the first edition, and I trust that they will find that this second edition represents an improvement. Finally I am very grateful to all my students at the Harvey Grammar School and at the Politics Association Revision Weeks who have remained uncomplaining as I bounced ideas off them, and who have learned not to wince at the phrase, "as you'll find in the book."

The following polling organisations have given permission for their findings to be used:

The Harris Research Centre (October 1974)
MORI (1979, 1983, 1987 and 1992)
National Opinion Polls (1970 and February 1974)
Social Surveys (Gallup Poll) Ltd. (1987, 1992 and monthly polls in *The Daily Telegraph*)

The following people have kindly allowed me to cite their work:
Les Back and John Solomos: *Who Represents Us?* (Birkbeck College Research Paper No. 3)

Professor Ivor Crewe (work on the 'new' and 'old' working class)

Patrick Dunleavy, Helen Margetts and Stuart Weir: *Replaying the 1992 General Election* (LSE Public Policy Paper No. 3)

The Hansard Society for Parliamentary Government: *Agenda for Change* and *Women at the Top*.

Frank Conley
Folkestone, Kent

1

Introduction: The electoral system

The British electoral system as we know it dates in its essentials from the late Victorian and Edwardian period, the fifty years up to the end of the First World War. The Reform Act of 1867 gave the vote to the men of the urban working class, appropriately described by Benjamin Disraeli as "leap in the dark" since no one knew quite what the consequences might be. Such a large number of new voters needed to be organised and motivated, particularly once the introduction of compulsory state education in 1870 meant that the electorate would be literate. This led to the establishment of party organisations, growing out of the registration societies set up in the early 1860s: the Conservatives created the National Union in 1867 and Central Office in 1870, followed by the National Liberal Federation in 1877. Voting by secret ballot was introduced in 1872, removing the fear of coercion and establishing the method of counting the votes, and the Corrupt and Illegal Practices Act of 1883 laid down the rules by which candidates' expenditure is still governed. Gladstone's Midlothian campaigns of 1879 and 1880 laid the foundations of modern campaigning, to the disgust of many, including Queen Victoria, who complained of "democratic rule".

The further extension of the franchise in 1884 also involved the creation of single-member constituencies in most parts of the United Kingdom. In 1892 Keir Hardie was the first MP to sit as a Labour member, and the Independent Labour Party was

"Grandma, you must let Vera vote for whom she chooses."
© Express Newspapers plc

set up in Bradford in the following year. In 1900 the Labour
Representation Committee incorporated the various bodies seeking
to put working-class members into parliament, the decision in
1911 to pay MPs removed a major obstacle to further growth in
the Labour movement, and in 1918 the split between supporters
of Asquith and Lloyd George in the Liberal Party created a gap
which Labour were well-placed to fill. In the same year the
principle was conceded that women should have the vote, and

state registration of voters, free postage and free hire of rooms was introduced. The only significant changes since then have been the extensions of the franchise in 1928 to women over 21 and in 1969 to all voters over 18.

For an electoral system to survive largely intact for so long without coming under extreme pressure or leading to corruption on the scale seen recently in Japan and Italy argues that it must have some positive advantages. On the other hand those who favour reform argue that the system has failed to adapt to political and demographic changes, so that it is no longer truly representative, and discriminates significantly against some groups. The issue of reform is discussed in the final chapter: this chapter considers whether the system is in fact biased in various ways, and some of the other peculiarities which have either been there from the beginning or have developed with age.

The first, and most obvious characteristic is that ours is a two-party system where the dominance of the parties of government, Conservative and Labour since the Second World War, is exaggerated by the voting system. There has only been one occasion since 1945 (and only two others since 1918) when a General Election has failed to produce an overall majority of seats for one party, yet in no General Election has any party had more than half the vote. The nearest any party has come to it was 1955, when the Conservatives had 49.7%: this was also the only occasion when the winning party had more than the next two parties combined (Labour and the Liberals together had 49.1%). Labour's highest was 48.8% in 1951, when they lost to the Conservatives. Since 1970 the Conservatives have never had more than 46.4%, and Labour's highest has been 39.3% in October 1974.

The "two-party" vote (Conservative and Labour combined) has shown a marked decline in the period since 1970. Before then the two main parties had between 87% and 97% of the vote; since then the highest was 81% in 1979, with the lowest being in the following general election, 1983, when Labour's showing resulted in a two-party vote of 70%. The extent to which the British electoral system distorts the outcome is shown by comparing the share of the vote with the share of the seats (Figure 1.1). Only once since 1945 have the two parties had less than 93% of the seats between them, and their share has usually been between 93% and 99%. Though this share declined at the same time as the share of the vote, the fall has been minute by comparison: in 1983, for example, the other parties had 30% of the vote but less than 7% of the seats.

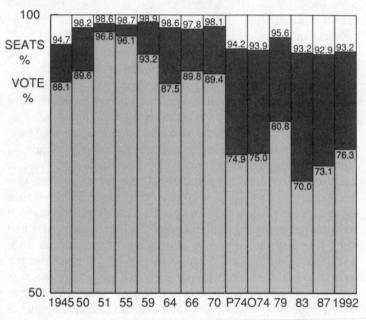

Figure 1.1 "Two-party" votes and seats

The distortion becomes even more marked when turnout is taken into account (Figure 1.2). This was at its highest in the 1950s, but apart from 1950 and 1951 it has been about 3% either side of 75%, with the low point coming in 1970. Taken in conjunction with the decline in the two-party vote it means that a declining proportion of the electorate supports the major parties (Table 1.1): in 1951 virtually 80% of the electorate voted either Conservative or Labour, whereas in 1983 under 51% did so.

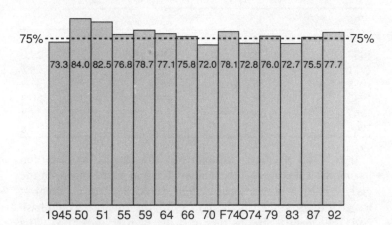

75% -75%

| 73.3 | 84.0 | 82.5 | 76.8 | 78.7 | 77.1 | 75.8 | 72.0 | 78.1 | 72.8 | 76.0 | 72.7 | 75.5 | 77.7 |

1945 50 51 55 59 64 66 70 F74O74 79 83 87 92

Figure 1.2 Turnout in General Elections, 1945–1992

Table 1.1   *Two-party vote as a percentage of the electorate*

Election	%	Election	%
1945	64.6	1970	64.4
1950	75.3	1974 (Feb.)	58.5
1951	79.9	1974 (Oct.)	54.6
1955	73.8	1979	61.4
1959	73.3	1983	50.9
1964	67.5	1987	55.2
1966	68.1	1992	58.8

This also applies to governments, of course. In 1955 the Conservatives had the support of 38% of the electorate. The two Labour governments elected in 1974 had 29% and 28.5% of the electorate, and in their last two successes the Conservatives have had 32.8% and 32.6% of those entitled to vote (Table 1.2). The fact that over two-thirds of those entitled to vote do not positively support the government in power raises interesting constitutional questions about the doctrine of the mandate.

Table 1.2   *Government support as a percentage of the electorate*

Election	%	Election	%
1945	35.4	1970	33.4
1950	38.7	1974 (Feb.)	29.0
1951	39.6	1974 (Oct.)	28.5
1955	38.2	1979	33.4
1959	38.9	1983	30.8
1964	34.0	1987	32.8
1966	36.3	1992	32.6

It is barely necessary to point out how much this distortion harms the Liberals and their allies. Even at their lowest, in the early 1950s, a proportional system would have given them at least 16 seats: at their highest, in 1983, the Alliance would have had 162, against the 23 they actually won (Figure 1.3). The reason for this is that the British electoral system favours concentration of votes and penalises those parties whose votes are spread evenly, particularly in terms of region. In the 1950s this worked in the Liberals' favour: in any system where there is a lower limit to qualify for seats, such as Germany, where 5% of the vote is needed to gain any party seats, or France, where candidates must have 12.5% to go into the second ballot, the Liberals would have disappeared, and might have ceased to exist as a national party. As it was, they still held on to a handful of seats in the "Celtic fringe". Since then, the system has worked against them. Their support is even in classes, age and sex as well as region, as discussed below, which means that they waste a great many votes in coming second, for which there are no prizes. By contrast the Conservatives and Labour can afford to come a poor third in hundreds of seats in the knowledge that there are at least 200 seats which are safe for each party. The lowest number of seats won by the Conservatives was 213 in 1945, that for Labour 209 in 1983. This characteristic was well illustrated in the 1979 election, when the Electoral Reform Society published a list of 400 "results" on polling day, most of them confirmed by the actual outcome: significantly none of the safe seats was held by the Liberals.

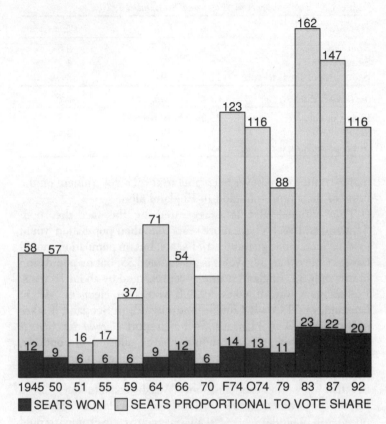

Figure 1.3 Liberal/Alliance seats, 1945–1992

Regional bias is well illustrated by Wales and Scotland, as is shown in Table 1.3. Labour is significantly over-represented in both regions, and the Conservatives under-represented. In Wales the Liberals are penalised, while Plaid Cymru benefit: in Scotland the situation is reversed, with the Liberals fairly treated by the system and the Scottish National Party severely under-represented. Labour's over-representation is important in view of their dependence on seats in Wales and Scotland to gain a

Table 1.3   *Party support in Wales and Scotland, 1992*

Wales (38 seats)	Cons	Lab	Lib	Plaid Cymru
Share of vote	28.6	49.5	12.4	8.8
Seats won	6	27	1	4
Seats proportional to vote	11	19	5	3

Scotland (72 seats)	Cons	Lab	Lib	SNP
Share of vote	25.7	39.0	13.1	21.5
Seats won	11	49	9	3
Seats proportional to vote	19	28	9	15

majority: they have never been able to form a government on the basis of their representation in England alone.

This regional bias is exaggerated by the fact that both Scotland and Wales have more seats than their population would justify. Scotland is guaranteed 71 seats, but on population should have no more than 59: Wales is guaranteed 35, but on population merits only 33. England is under-represented by about 18 seats. Put another way, it takes 69,000 voters to elect an MP in England, or 71,000 if London is excluded; in Scotland it takes only 54,000. The Hansard Society report *Agenda for Change* argued that this anomaly should not be allowed to continue, since the arguments about constituencies being too large if they included a population near the average apply to only seven Scottish constituencies and one Welsh constituency, but a Labour government would obviously be unwilling to reduce its number of potential seats, and a Conservative government would run into accusations of gerrymandering.

The guarantees of seats to Scotland and Wales (and to Northern Ireland, whose 17 seats are appropriate to the population) derive from the legislation relating to boundary changes. This is a relatively new feature in the British system, dating in its essentials only from 1948. There are four boundary commissions, one for each of the regions: as well as the guaranteed minimum, they are bound to ensure that the seats are roughly equal in number of voters and to take account of local government and geographical boundaries. Originally they were expected to review boundaries every three to seven years, but the intervals have got much wider, and the two most significant revisions took place in the late 1960s and the early 1980s. Because Labour has had a disproportionate number of relatively small constituencies in the cities, they are more likely to lose through mergers, just as the Conservatives gain from the creation of new seats in the growing areas of the south and east where they are strongest. As well as reducing the actual number of seats held, there is a likelihood that boundary reviews reduce the number of marginals available to parties seeking to win office. On the other hand Labour benefits as time goes on, and people move from Labour areas into Conservative ones, thus renewing the bias in their favour until the next review. In any case, the evidence suggests that the requirements to respect existing local boundaries mean that Labour does not lose as many as strict numerical considerations would suggest.

Even at the outset, the Labour Home Secretary who intro-duced the first boundary reviews was criticised by his own side, and in 1969 James Callaghan, Home Secretary in another Labour government, introduced the latest proposals to Parliament with a strong hint that Labour members should vote to delay them, so that the new boundaries first operated in February 1974 and may have contributed to the indecisive result. In 1983 Labour, by then in opposition, challenged the boundary review in the courts, unsuccessfully, in the belief that it would cost them 20–30 seats. In view of the collapse of the Labour vote in the subsequent General Election it is difficult to assess the extent to which Labour lost through the review, but it is estimated that the next review will cost Labour a further 12 seats at least. This would have been bad enough after the next General Election in 1996 or 1997, but immediately after the 1992 election the government announced its intention to bring the implementation of the review forward, thus undermining Labour's hopes of achieving enough additional seats to form a government.

As well as the possible bias caused by constituency boundaries, there is the wider question of inbuilt bias in the electoral system

©Private Eye

for one major party or the other. The evidence is not really conclusive. In the 1950s it was assumed that Labour wasted more votes. Thus in 1950 an even split of the vote between Conservatives and Labour would have put the Conservatives 35 ahead, and in 1959 Labour would have needed 1.4% more of the vote than the Conservatives to gain the same number of seats. By 1964 this bias seemed to have disappeared: an even split of the vote would have given the Conservatives only one extra seat, and in 1966 Labour would have been 22 ahead on an even split. By October 1974 the anti-Labour bias seemed to have returned. On the average swing of 2.2% Labour should have taken 25 from the Conservatives, giving them an overall majority of 17: instead they took only 17 for a majority of 3. It was assumed that this had something to do with the Conservatives putting an extra effort into super-marginal seats, but this would not explain those occasions such as 1992 when the bias appeared to work the other way.

The whole concept of "swing", the movement of votes from one party to another, has caused increasing problems in recent elections, which suggests that the system is behaving in more unpredictable ways. In 1950 David Butler put forward the

"Cube Law", which he had discovered in minutes of evidence to a Royal Commission on Electoral Systems in 1910. According to this, if the votes were divided between the two major parties in the ratio A:B, then seats would divide in the ratio $A^3:B^3$. Thus for every 1% swing, about 3% of seats (about 18) would change. This worked beautifully for all general elections from 1931 to 1970, but then things started to go wrong: in 1974 only 12 seats changed on a 1% swing, and in 1983 only 9. From being a Cube Law, it had become a Law of the Power of 1.6, as David Butler has put it. If the Cube Law had worked in 1987 as it did in 1959 the Conservatives would have had 450 seats, not 376. In 1992 it became worse still. If the Cube Law had worked, the Conservatives would have had 390 to Labour's 217, instead of the split being 336 to 271.

The General Elections after 1970 show particularly that general assumptions about "swing" are no longer valid. It was always based on votes moving between the two major parties, and was calculated by adding the percentage loss for one party to the percentage gain for the other and dividing by two. Thus in 1970 the Conservatives gained about 4.5% and Labour lost 4.9%, giving a swing of 4.7%. This was always too simple to be wholly reliable, and became less and less valid as third parties became more prominent in the electoral arithmetic. Boundary changes and regional variations throughout the period from 1974 to 1992 added to the difficulty of predicting anything useful from two-party swing, and the failure of the BBC's revived Swingometer in 1992 in the face of wide variations even between adjacent constituencies should have seen the end of such simplistic generalisations about electoral behaviour, whatever may have been the case in the past.

Apologists for the British system concede many of the problems and distortions, but argue that it is representative in a more general way, in reflecting the wishes of the electorate for a quick, decisive result and the opportunity to get rid of an unpopular government with a fairly small movement of votes. Certainly the result is quick, particularly in these days of computer analysis. Only in February 1974 was the result delayed by more than a few hours, and in 1983 and 1987 a reliable estimate was available within minutes of the polls closing. Even the surprise result in 1992 was undoubted by breakfast time on 10 April, though the technical mark of 326 seats was not passed until early afternoon.

The second assumption is a myth, though it is one with a pedigree at least as far back as the nineteenth-century Prime Minister Lord Salisbury, who talked of "the great law of the Pendulum". Certainly our system shows when a party has lost support on a large scale, as the Conservatives found in 1945, 1964 and 1974, and Labour in 1970 and 1983. Yet there has not been a General Election since 1970 where a majority for one party has been transformed into a majority for the other. In practice our system more often produces long periods of domination for one party. In the nineteenth century the Conservatives did not have an overall majority between 1846 and 1874: between 1918 and 1945 there were less than four years (1924 and 1929–1931) when the government did not consist of Conservatives or Conservative-dominated coalitions. In the period since 1945 the pendulum seems to have got stuck more often than not (Figure 1.4). The Conservatives held office for 13 years from 1951 to 1964; Labour were in power for 11 of the next 15 years; by the time of the next general election the Conservatives will have formed the government for at least 17 years. The only element of truth in this is the effect of a small number of votes. In 1964 Labour would have lost if 900 of their voters had voted differently or abstained: in 1992 if 1,100 voters had not voted Conservative there would have been a hung Parliament.

The final question to be asked in deciding whether the British electoral system is genuinely representative is whether it reflects the nature of society. There is no need, nor space, to discuss whether Parliament is representative by occupations, but fortunately there are two aspects which are easier to assess: the representation of women and ethnic minorities. Even though women have had the vote since 1918 and the first woman entered Parliament soon afterwards, at a by-election in 1919, the number of women in Parliament has always been small: the election of 60 women in 1992 was a record. Even so, at just over

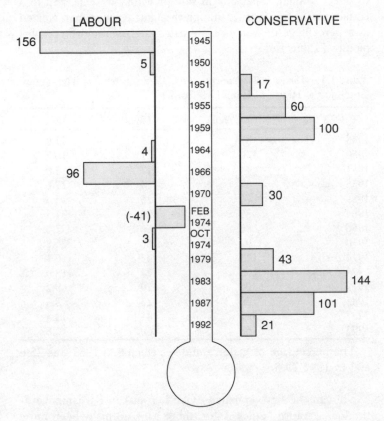

Figure 1.4 The "pendulum": majorities, 1945–1992

9% this is one of the lowest in Europe. In 1990 the Hansard Society report *Women at the Top* found that only France had a lower ratio of men to women among the eleven main European democracies, and the four Scandinavian countries each had over 30% of women Members of Parliament, with Sweden the highest at 38% (133 women from a total of 349). At that stage Britain's percentage was 6.3%.

The usual explanation is that constituency parties are reluctant to select women, especially in safe or winnable seats, and to a certain extent this is true, though the figures for women elected as a percentage of women candidates suggest a more complex picture (Table 1.4).

Table 1.4 *Women in Parliament, 1945–1992 (figures from* The Times Guide to the House of Commons April 1992)

	Candidates	Elected	Percentage
1945	87	24	27.6
1950	126	21	16.7
1951	74	17	23.0
1955	87	24	27.6
1959	75	25	33.3
1964	89	28	31.5
1966	80	26	32.5
1970	97	26	26.8
1974 (Feb.)	143	23	16.1
1974 (Oct.)	150	27	18.0
1979	206	19	9.2
1983	276	23	8.3
1987	327	41	12.5
1992	568	60	10.6

The percentage of male candidates elected in 1987 was 25.6 and in 1992 29.6.

Though the first woman to take her seat in Parliament was the Conservative Nancy Astor, there have normally been more Labour MPs among the women elected: in 1987 there were 21 Labour to 17 Conservatives, and in 1992 37 Labour to 20 Conservatives. Only in 1970 was the balance the other way, with 15 Conservatives to 10 Labour. Labour has taken more positive steps to increase the number of women in Parliament by insisting that there must be at least one woman on any shortlist. In addition the all-party 300 Group is committed to a more appropriate balance between men and women, and at least 100 women in the House of Commons by the end of the decade. Time will tell whether the increase in the number of women candidates in the last three general elections will be matched by an increase in the number who are successful.

Four MPs were elected from ethnic minorities in 1987, three of them in London and all of them Labour. In 1992 they were joined by the Conservative Nirj Deva in Brentford and Isleworth and the Labour MP Piara Khabra in Ealing Southall, though Ashok Kumar failed to hang on to his seat at Langbaurgh, won for Labour in a by-election. It seems likely that candidate selection is again the reason for the low number of minority candidates elected. Some light is shed on this by the case study carried out in Birmingham Small Heath by two lecturers at Birkbeck College, Les Back and John Solomos. This showed that in spite of a significant number of black Labour councillors on Birmingham City Council, Labour has yet to select a black candidate for one of its safe Labour seats in the city, and in Small Heath a white candidate was selected even though about half the population comes from Pakistan, Kashmir in particular and 90% of constituency Labour Party members from the same region. This is not the place to debate the rights and wrongs of this particular selection, but in the General Election the Conservatives put up an Asian candidate and recorded a swing to them of 2.5%, against the trend in the rest of Birmingham, though since Labour's majority was still nearly 14,000 this is hardly significant. Labour's processes for selecting candidates have been under review for some time, but it will almost certainly take a number of general elections for constituency parties of all types to change their ways of thinking about the suitability of candidates. This was exemplified for the Conservatives in Cheltenham, where there was great controversy over the selection of the black barrister John Taylor, who lost the seat to the Liberals with a swing of over 5%. It will take longer still for there to be significant change from the white, middle-class male predominance in the House of Commons which the electoral system currently produces.

2

General Elections, 1945–1959

There were five General Elections in the fourteen years following the end of the Second World War: in 1945, 1950, 1951, 1955 and 1959. Labour held office from 1945 to 1951 under one Prime Minister, Clement Attlee: the Conservatives were in power for the remainder, as indeed they were to be until 1964, under three Prime Ministers, Winston Churchill, Anthony Eden and Harold Macmillan.

Many of the features now taken for granted in General Elections first appeared during this period. The first of the "Nuffield" election studies, by R. B. McCallum and Alison Readman, appeared after the 1945 Election, which also saw the first significant use of opinion polls, first used in a British by-election in Fulham in 1938. Television first played a small part in 1955 and a much greater one in 1959, and in the same election the Conservatives first made use of an advertising agency. Many of the themes to be seen in more recent elections were apparent, such as the role of leaders, the capacity of parties to lose elections from apparently winning positions or to recover from seeming disasters, and the significance or otherwise of the campaign. It is these themes that will emerge as each General Election is considered, as well as the background, campaign and results.

1945

The previous General Election had been in 1935, and had given an enormous majority to the National Government, made up principally of Conservatives, who had 585 seats. Labour were determined that the wartime coalition should not continue longer than necessary: they had no intention of allowing Churchill to prolong the coalition in the way in which Lloyd George had done in 1918. Thus some in the Labour Party were seriously considering quitting the coalition in September 1944, though the Labour leader, Attlee, opposed this; their draft manifesto was approved by the National Executive Committee in January 1945; and they refused to agree to Churchill's proposal on 18 May, ten days after the end of the war in Europe, that the coalition should go on at least until the end of the war against Japan, a decision enthusiastically endorsed by the Labour Conference. Thus Polling Day was set for 5 July.

The Conservative campaign (which they fought under the "National" banner) concentrated almost entirely on Churchill. Posters urged voters to "let him finish the job", and he made four of the party's ten radio broadcasts. His personal popularity remained high, confirmed by the triumphal nature of his reception as he travelled around the country, and there were many who believed that he would still be Prime Minister even if Labour won, in spite of Churchill's warnings to the contrary in his last broadcast. Anthony Eden was one of a fairly small number of Conservatives who saw this as a mistake. He wrote that they had fought the campaign badly in trying to win on Churchill's personality instead of a programme: the modern electorate was too intelligent for that and disliked being talked down to. While there was a great deal of gratitude to Churchill as wartime leader, there was not the same enthusiasm for him as Prime Minister for the peace.

The most controversial aspect of Churchill's involvement came with an election broadcast on 4 June in which he claimed that a Labour government would mean totalitarianism and an erosion of savings, and specifically referred to a "Gestapo" of civil servants. Although these ideas have been attributed to Lord Beaverbrook, they seem to have been Churchill's own. Churchill later told Eden that he might not have made the remarks if Eden had been there to advise him, but even

Conservatives such as R. A. Butler saw the broadcast as a great strategic blunder.

Attlee was quick to seize on these comments: in his own broadcast of the following day he thanked Churchill for making explicit the difference between "Winston Churchill the great leader in war of a united nation and Mr Churchill the Party Leader of the Conservatives", a point also made by the cartoonist David Low. Churchill had failed to take account of two important assets for Labour. The first was that their involvement in the wartime coalition had shown that they could cope with the demands of government; indeed Attlee had frequently deputised for Churchill in the House of Commons and elsewhere, and had become much better known as a result. More important was the general mood that it was time for a change, and that this would not come from the Conservatives. To a great extent this had been been fuelled by the publication in 1942 of the Beveridge Report on Social Insurance and Allied Services, which not only held out the hope of a better future, it provided a detailed blueprint. Many were disappointed by the government's luke-warm response at the time, and their failure to make specific commitments in their 1945 manifesto. For many, too, this would be their first opportunity to vote, since there had not been a General Election for ten years.

Voting and the count took nearly three weeks because of holiday weeks in some towns and the fact that many voters were still in the Forces. Few Conservatives, except Eden, expected to lose, and Churchill predicted a majority between 30 and 80. The turnout was the lowest before 1970 at 73.3%, and after the result the Conservatives believed that this helped them to lose, but the scale of the Labour victory (Table 2.1), on a par with the Liberal success in 1906, was too great to be explained solely by low turnout.

This was the first time that Labour had secured a larger share of the vote than the Conservatives, and meant that they were able to embark on their radical programme for social reform and public ownership without the need for the support of any other party.

Two Churchills
© John Appleton, Solo Syndication and Literary Agency
Source: Cartoon Study Centre, University of Kent, Canterbury (Sir
    David Low, *Evening Standard*, 31 July 1945)

Table 2.1 *Scale of Labour victory, 1945*

	Seats	Votes
Labour	393	48.3%
Conservative	213	39.8%
Liberals	12	9.1% (300 candidates)
Others	22	2.8%
Labour majority	146 (640 seats)	

1950

The period from 1945 to 1950 divides into two. Before 1949
Labour had everything their own way, thanks in large measure
to the decisiveness and skill of Attlee. His reputation is now so
secure that it is surprising to realise that in 1945 many, including
Harold Laski and Stafford Cripps, supported his replacement
by Herbert Morrison, and it took the intervention of Ernest
Bevin to secure Attlee's position as leader and to fend off Laski's
rather impertinent attempts to insist that the Prime Minister
ought to be subject to the dictates of Labour's NEC. Attlee
chose a Cabinet of wide range and ability, with Bevin as Foreign
Secretary, Morrison responsible for the nationalisation programme and Aneurin Bevan building on the work of Lloyd
George before the First World War and Neville Chamberlain in
the 1920s in giving practical expression to the Beveridge Report:
later Attlee was to describe the National Health Service a
his government's greatest single achievement in home affairs.
Crucially, Attlee was content largely to leave his ministers to get
on with the job once he had appointed them, as long as they
were capable: as his biographer has said, Attlee is the only Prime
Minister this century to come to Downing Street with a well-
considered view of the nature of the job, the demands of Cabinet
government and the best method of running an administration.

By contrast with Labour's elation and sense of mission after
their 1945 success, the Conservatives were initially stunned by
their loss: if Churchill could not win, who could? Churchill
himself saw his defeat as a betrayal, and bitterly rejected the
Order of the Garter on the grounds that the people had already
given him the order of the boot. The problem was not only that
he was old and tired, he had never been Leader of the
Opposition and was not interested in the day-to-day detail of
opposing a government, more in the grand sweep of the crusade
against socialism which he had been waging since 1917. In
addition he was committed to writing his war memoirs, of which
the first volume of six appeared in April 1948. There was no
organised Shadow Cabinet in the modern sense, and in any case

the Conservatives largely accepted much of the social legislation: the government had more trouble from the British Medical Association than from the official opposition.

The problems began to get serious in the spring of 1949. There had been difficulties with the balance of payments since 1945, and the 1949 budget saw a continuation of the wages and prices policy. Although the Conservatives did not win a single by-election during this parliament, they made substantial gains in local elections in 1949, and the dock strike which began in May suggested that the government had lost its grip on industrial relations. Attlee was convinced of the need for devaluation of the pound by July, but Cripps, the Chancellor, resisted until the last moment before announcing a devaluation from $4.03 to $2.80 in September. This was followed by a package of economic measures in October which included defence cuts and 1/- (5p) on prescriptions.

Attlee decided on 23 February 1950 as polling day rather than waiting until June. The decision took Churchill by surprise: he was out of England when the election was announced, and only turned his attention to the manifesto when he returned. He described the campaign as demure and sedate, and it was largely dominated by the party managers and front benchers. The only significant issue was nationalisation. The Conservatives were pledged to return the steel industry to the private sector while Labour were committed to extending the public sector, so that the Conservatives were able to claim the result as a rejection of this policy.

In point of fact the result was unsatisfactory and disappointing to all parties (Table 2.2). The turnout was 84%, still the highest post-war figure, which produced the ironic situation that Labour's number of votes was their highest ever and the highest so far achieved by any party (13.3 million) but their share of the vote and their seats were sharply lower. The Conservatives had expected to win, based on the hardening of middle-class opposition to Labour, on boundary changes, which had probably cost Labour between 30 and 35 seats including the disappearance of 19 of the 62 seats in the solid Labour London County Council

Table 2.2   *General Election result, 1950*

	Seats	Votes
Labour	315	46.1%
Conservative	299	43.5%
Liberals	9	9.1%
Others	21	1.3%
Labour majority	5 (625 seats)	

area, and on the probable gain of 10 seats from the postal vote. Certainly their votes and seats rose, but not enough. The Liberals had fielded far more candidates than in 1945 (475) and their share of the vote was the same, but they lost three seats in comparison with 1945.

After some discussion about an all-party conference, Attlee decided to form another Labour government, but the small majority meant that another election was inevitable before long.

1951

The balance between government and opposition was completely reversed after the 1950 General Election. Whereas before it Labour had been buoyed up by their sense of mission and the Conservatives were depressed, afterwards the government was led by sick and harassed men, in the words of one writer, and the new Conservative intake were determined to make life as difficult as possible, forcing Labour to bring in members from hospital to vote in order to avoid defeat. Attlee himself, now aged 67, was not in the best of health, but was still seen by many as the party's best asset, helping to restrain the extremists. The team which had been so successful before 1950 was breaking up. Cripps resigned as Chancellor in October 1950, and was replaced by a younger figure, Hugh Gaitskell. More seriously, Ernest Bevin was dying. Attlee had relied heavily on him in managing his Cabinet, knowing that if he had Bevin's approval the rest of the Cabinet would follow suit. There is disagreement among recent writers as to Attlee's treatment of

Bevin. Some say that he was brusquely forced from the post of Foreign Secretary when his illness became plain, but Attlee's official biographer says that he was moved to a relative sinecure, and that the only possible criticism of Attlee is that he left Bevin at the Foreign Office too long. Certainly Bevin was dead within five weeks of resigning as Foreign Secretary. His replacement, Herbert Morrison, was a disaster, "the worst appointment I ever made" in Attlee's own words. Finally Aneurin Bevan, who had threatened to resign in 1950 over prescription charges and his fear that NHS policy was being determined by the Treasury, actually did so in April 1951, taking with him two younger men, Harold Wilson and John Freeman.

There were further problems. The Korean War enhanced Attlee's personal standing, but it undermined economic recovery, and there were serious difficulties over the nationalisation of Iranian oil-fields. In the midst of the crisis Attlee announced that Parliament would be dissolved on 5 October and polling day would be on 25 October. It has been said that this was an unexpected decision by Attlee. It may have seemed so to outsiders, but Attlee had been considering it since Bevan's resignation and wrote to Morrison at the end of May suggesting October: the reason was that the King was scheduled to visit Australia and New Zealand early in 1952, and Attlee thought it only fair for the new government to be established before he left. The claim of an unexpected decision seems to derive from Morrison, who opposed October and may not have been happy at being disregarded.

The Conservatives had every reason to feel confident. The only slight problem was Churchill, who was 75 and had suffered a mild stroke in August 1949, but by July 1951 Harold Macmillan described him as on tremendous form, with a complete ascendancy over the party and the House of Commons. Otherwise everything was indisputably in their favour. The new intake of able young men had created a positive alternative to socialism, and they were not associated with post-war austerity and controls. The post-war overhaul of the party organisation was starting to pay dividends: it was estimated that their Central Office staff of over two hundred was more than double Labour's staff at Transport House. The Conservatives were comfortably ahead in the polls by October: by contrast Labour's position got worse the longer they stayed in office, with Attlee's personal rating falling from 57% in May to 44% in September.

The campaign was low-key, with the Conservatives attacking Labour's domestic record on rising prices and housing shortages. They were ahead on every domestic issue except employment, in spite of the accusation in *The Times* that the Conservative campaign was designed not to lose votes rather than gain them. The only controversial episode was the *Daily Mirror*'s "Whose finger on the trigger?" headline, which may have caused a slight swing back to Labour. Certainly the result was not as decisive as the Conservatives had hoped (Table 2.3), with a swing of only 1.1% in their favour, so that they were fairly relieved to have got back at all. The turnout was down slightly at 82.5%, but both the major parties saw their share of the vote rise sharply at the expense of the Liberals. Their performance was their worst post-war: they had only 109 candidates and 2.5% of the vote, down from 3 million in 1950 to 730,000, but still kept 6 seats. Labour had more votes than the Conservatives, and indeed had the highest number of votes for any party, 13.9 million, until 1992, but had 26 fewer seats. If nothing else, the 1951 General Election showed how peculiar the British electoral system can be.

Table 2.3 *General Election result, 1951*

	Seats	Votes
Conservative	321	48.0%
Labour	295	48.8%
Liberal	6	2.5%
Others	3	0.7%
Conservative majority	17 (625 seats)	

1955

There are many reasons why the Parliament from 1951 to 1955 was comparatively uneventful and low-key. From one point of

Hot seat
© John Appleton, Solo Syndication and Literary Agency
Source: Cartoon Study Centre, University of Kent, Canterbury (Sir
David Low, *Daily Herald*, 30 October 1951)

view, all the government had to do was to sit tight and ride as
both the international and national scene improved. Stalin's
death, the end of the Korean War, the Coronation in 1953 and
the removal of the last post-war controls created a mood of
optimism not seen since the end of the war. On the other hand
there was a danger of drift, partly caused by the small majority,

partly by Churchill's feeling that Britain needed several years of quiet and steady administration.

The main problem for the Conservatives was when Churchill was going to retire. Originally he had talked of going after a year, but he always could find reasons to stay. Criticism had started by April 1952, and at the beginning of 1953 Harry Crookshank, the Leader of the House, was claiming that the Conservatives would have had 60 more seats without Churchill. Eden was seriously ill in April 1953, and the strain of handling the Foreign Office as well the premiership and the Coronation helped to cause Churchill's serious stroke in June. It is impossible to say whether Churchill might have gone then if Eden had been fully fit, but the relationship never recovered, Eden believing that he was not trusted, and Churchill complaining in August 1954 that he was being hounded out because his second-in-command wanted the job, and seriously talking of leading the Conservatives into the next General Election. Eventually he stepped down in April 1955, during a newspaper strike, claiming, possibly tongue-in-cheek, that no two men had ever changed guard more smoothly.

Labour had also been having problems of a similar nature concerning Attlee. He was afraid that if he retired, Morrison would succeed him: meanwhile Bevan had resigned from the shadow cabinet over German rearmament, effectively creating two oppositions. Fortunately the most bitter disputes took place in secret. On the other hand their claims that there would be problems under the Conservatives had proved unfounded, and there was little or no reason for voters to change their allegiance.

Churchill retired on 6 April; on the 15th Eden asked for Parliament to be dissolved on 6 May, and polling day was set for 26 May. The veteran Labour politician Hugh Dalton described the 1955 campaign as the dullest of the twelve he had fought. Neither party made many promises, and apart from a few marginal seats there was little interest. In spite of his colleagues' initial doubts, Eden fought a very effective personal campaign, making the most of his undoubted popularity, and earned the approval of both Churchill and Macmillan. For the first time ministers and others appeared on television to explain their policies. Churchill was not impressed: he cancelled a proposed broadcast, and said that a candidate should make "a pronouncement that will become a part of the English language, part of English history. People ought to have to fight to get into his meetings." There is no evidence that television altered the outcome in any significant way.

The turnout continued to fall, down to 76.8%, representing 2 million votes less than in 1951, but the Conservatives' share of the vote and their seats went up again, though their number of votes was 412,000 less. Their share of the vote was their highest ever, the highest for any party before or since, the first time since 1935 that they had had more than Labour, and the only time that they have had more than Labour or Liberals combined (Table 2.4). It was the first time for ninety years that they or any party had increased their vote share from one general election to the next. Labour had lost over 1.5 million votes since 1951, but the Liberals had slightly increased their share of the vote in keeping the same number of seats.

Table 2.4 *General Election result, 1955*

	Seats	*Votes*
Conservative	345	49.7%
Labour	277	46.4%
Liberal	6	2.7%
Others	2	1.2%
Conservative majority	60 (630 seats)	

1959

In common with more recent general elections, that of 1959 confirms the ability of a government to recover from near-disasters, especially if they change their leader. The problems for Eden began almost at once. As a politician he had virtually no experience outside foreign affairs, and had turned down Churchill's suggestion in 1952 that he might take a greater role

in home policy: as a person he was aloof, and found it difficult
to run a Cabinet. In the autumn of 1955 a tough budget
including rises in purchase tax was introduced to curb the
inflation increased by pre-election tax cuts. In December 1955
the Torbay by-election saw the Conservative vote fall by 9.4%,
a disaster by the standards of the time, and by the spring of 1956
Eden's personal popularity was down from a peak of 70% to
40% in one opinion poll. The situation was not improved when
Butler's opinion of Eden as "the best Prime minister we've got"
was quoted out of context.

Then came the Suez crisis. There is no need to go into detail
here, but the controversy split families and friendships in a way
which had not been seen since the Munich Agreement of 1938.
Two ministers resigned, and the Conservative Party was split. In
October 1956 Eden's health gave way and he went to convalesce
in Jamaica. On his return it was clear that he had lost most of
his authority with the Party and the House of Commons and
though colleagues urged him to stay, he resigned within a few
weeks.

There were two contenders for the leadership. R. A. Butler
had been running the government during Eden's absence, and
so was to a certain extent tainted: in addition he was seen in
some quarters as unsound, with a tendency to let his tongue run
away with him. Harold Macmillan, on the other hand, had
overcome the jibe that he had been "first in and first out" over
Suez, and was seen as calm and responsible. Although opinion
polls and the press expected Butler to succeed Eden, only one
member of the Cabinet supported him.

Macmillan only expected to last six weeks, until the House of
Commons debate on Suez. In fact the government had a
majority of 49, and Macmillan seemed to have a knack of
overcoming problems such as by-election reverses and resignations, including the three Treasury ministers in January 1958,
which he dismissed as "a little local difficulty".

In the Labour party, Attlee had wanted to resign immediately
after the 1955 defeat, but stayed until December, allowing Hugh
Gaitskell to secure the leadership instead of Bevan or Morrison.

According to his colleague George Brown, Gaitskell aimed to modernise and refashion the Labour Party as an instrument of appeal to all sections of society, but although the divisions with the Bevanites had been patched up there were still problems. Gaitskell's own image was austere, Labour's organisation was weak, with a loss of nearly a quarter of their full-time agents between 1951 and 1955, and there were policy disputes over nationalisation, with G. D. H. Cole and Richard Crossman calling for an extension of the public sector based on workers' control, and Gaitskell arguing at the 1957 Party Conference that nationalisation should only be an option for industries in trouble.

By this time the Conservatives were planning for the next General Election. They decided against October 1958 because of the impact of the new Rent Act and advised against October 1959 because sterling crises always seemed to happen in the autumn of odd-numbered years. The budget of 1959 was described by one economist as the most generous ever introduced in peacetime conditions with cuts in income tax and purchase tax and increased investment in housing and education. This added to the "feel-good" factor which Macmillan had described in July 1957 as "a state of prosperity such as we have never had in my lifetime – nor indeed ever in the history of this country." With a 7% lead in opinion polls, and successes in foreign affairs the Conservatives could safely risk an election on 8 October 1959.

The campaign surprised some by its vulgarity, but the most important thing was to win. As in subsequent elections the Conservatives saw their lead fall during the second and third weeks of the campaign, creating the fear that Gaitskell had made too good a start, but in fact there was never much reason for voters to change allegiance. Gaitskell was unwise enough to claim that Labour would increase welfare spending without raising taxes, only to be flattened by Macmillan's dismissive announcement that if this was an auction he was not in it. Macmillan travelled over 2,500 miles and addressed 74 meetings, and even his opponents conceded that his personality helped to win the election: his Gallup rating was 67%. Although the

© The Observer

Conservative campaign cost £500,000, and involved advice from people as diverse as Bud Flanagan and the novelist and broadcaster Norman Collins it looked stilted and awkward much of the time, especially in contrast with the professionalism of Labour's broadcasts. As Labour have found since, their skill in making effective television broadcasts gives them no advantage at all. One interesting use of television was that Gaitskell conceded defeat in an interview after barely 200 constituencies had declared.

The turnout was slightly above 1955 at 78.7%, and the Conservatives saw their number of seats rise in almost every region, though the swing to them was only 1.1% and their share of the vote was slightly down. Labour lost both seats and votes, and while the Liberals nearly doubled their share of the vote they did not increase their seats by comparison with 1955 (Table 2.5). Thus the Conservatives had achieved something they have not done since: they had increased their majority in three successive general elections.

Table 2.5   *General Election result, 1959*

	Seats	*Votes*
Conservatives	365	49.4%
Labour	258	43.8%
Liberals	6	5.9%
Other	1	0.9%
Conservative majority	100 (630 seats)	

3

The General Election of 1964

Background

The parliament which began in 1959 was the longest post-war, and showed three phases, though there were no clear points of division, let alone reasons why. To start with the Conservatives were riding high after their third successive victory: then a series of set-backs and disasters coincided with and helped a Labour revival to the extent that a large Labour victory seemed not only probable but inevitable; finally the Conservatives recovered enough for it to seem possible that they could still win.

The first phase saw the government apparently holding their own as Labour continued to encounter problems. In almost every by-election the Labour share of the vote fell, and where the Conservatives lost votes it was to the Liberals: by October 1960 50% of an opinion poll said that their opinion of Labour had fallen since the General Election. The main issue was defence, where Gaitskell had failed to overcome the union block vote supporting a unilateralist policy at the 1960 Conference, in spite of his impassioned plea to "fight, fight and fight again to save the party we love". The unions and the left also opposed plans to abandon Clause 4, and there was little support for Douglas Jay's proposal to change the party's name. As late as 1961 party leaders such as Anthony Crosland and neutral observers such as *The Times* were suggesting that it would take several elections to eat away the Conservative lead. On the other hand, the scale of the 1959 defeat had focused the minds of the Labour leadership on the need to plan for the future rather than look back to the past. A programme was agreed to concentrate on domestic policies and appeal to the new generation of voters. In October 1961 "Signposts for the Sixties" appeared, and was to form the basis of much of Labour's manifesto. The Party Conference saw the unilateralist decisions of the previous year reversed and agreement on a domestic programme embodied in "Signposts for the Sixties". Much of Labour's 1964 manifesto was subsequently based on this, and in the short term Gaitskell's reputation was substantially enhanced.

1961 saw the start of serious problems for the Conservatives. Looking back, Lord Hailsham detected a feeling of disunity in the party as early as the autumn, possibly caused by complacency among the new intake. More specifically the early summer saw severe pressure on sterling and a serious balance of payments deficit, which led to a special budget including a pay pause. This was deeply unpopular: within weeks, 49% thought that the Chancellor (Selwyn Lloyd, who had taken the job only reluctantly in 1960) was doing a bad job, and only 29% expected the proposals to succeed. Poll ratings for the Conservatives fell from 47% to 38%, the first time for three years that they had been behind Labour.

Calls for Macmillan to go began as early as February 1962, as his patrician, "laid-back" style began to seem more and more out of tune with the times. Six of his Cabinet had been to Eton, and only two had not been to independent schools. Of 85 members of the government, 35 were related to him: as Attlee commented, the daily prayer of Tory backbenchers ought to be "God bless our Mac and his relations, and keep us in our proper stations." In March 1962 the Conservatives suffered their worst by-election set-back since the war, losing the safe seat of Orpington to the Liberals. In July the Conservative candidate came third in Leicester North-East. These reverses convinced Macmillan that a new direction was needed, especially in the economy. For some reason he decided on a political bloodbath, dismissing a third of his Cabinet in one go. He later conceded that this was a mistake, and that he should have been content with changing the Chancellor. Even to colleagues this looked like panic, and one of his victims, the Lord Chancellor, Lord Kilmuir, accused him of losing both nerve and judgement.

For some time Macmillan had been using foreign affairs to provide success, culminating in an application to join the Common Market. This caused domestic difficulties, with a high proportion of people surveyed undecided and wanting an election on the issue, but the whole issue was settled, at least for the time being, by a French veto at the end of January 1963. At the same time Labour were showing clear signs of recovery, having won three seats from the Tories in the latter part of 1962. Sadly their leader, Hugh Gaitskell, was not to see the fruits of Labour's revival, dying suddenly in January 1963. His replacement was Harold Wilson, who brought a totally new style to political leadership which matched the popular desire for change. In the first place, he represented a new generation which had been born after the First World War: the equivalent figures had not yet reached the top in the Tory party. Equally important was his emphasis on the need for purposeful change based on the new opportunities provided by science and technology: his phrase "the white heat of the technological revolution" has now become a cliché, but at the time it offered a vision of progress similar to that promoted by Labour in 1945.

Wilson's combination of wit and venom in his parliamentary performances rocked the government back on their heels, and things became hugely worse as 1963 went on. A series of linked scandals involving call-girls, Russian diplomats and an osteopath also implicated the War Minister John Profumo, who was forced to resign. In spite of Hailsham's fulminations about "a woman of easy virtue and a proved liar", only 23% believed that Macmillan should stay, and 67% felt that security precautions had been inadequate. The issue of whether Macmillan should lead the party into the next election was settled in October 1963 when he was advised that his health would not allow him to continue. In later life he and others wondered whether he might not have recovered sufficiently from his prostate operation to go on, but it is difficult to believe that the Conservatives would have done any better with him in charge than they did, and they might well have done much worse.

The leadership contest made matters still worse for the government, at least to start with. This time Butler was expected to be successful, with the main challenge coming from the younger Reginald Maudling. This overlooked the fact that peers could now renounce their peerages, which enabled Lord Hailsham to become Quintin Hogg once again, and the Earl of Home, Macmillan's Foreign Secretary, to become Sir Alec Douglas-Home. Because the process by which the leader "emerged" was secret and informal it aroused great argument and bitterness. Macmillan's own instinct at the time was that Hailsham had the charisma necessary to meet Wilson on level terms, but that he was too volatile, as the later election campaign confirmed. According to his biographer he later wondered whether Butler might not have done a better job, but others have said that Macmillan's main aim was to keep Butler out and, in any case, Eden's description of Butler as "the artful dodger" was shared by many in the party. In the event Douglas-Home seemed to have the fewest enemies, and Macmillan advised the Queen to ask him to form a government. Even that caused problems, when Iain Macleod and Enoch Powell refused to serve, and the whole turmoil was kept going by the publication in 1964 of Randolph Churchill's book *The Fight for the Tory Leadership*.

The main difficulty for Douglas-Home was the lack of time in which to establish himself. Party managers complained that it had taken eighteen months to establish Macmillan after 1957, but the next General Election was less than a year away at most. Douglas-Home's background did not help: like Macmillan he was a product of Eton and Oxford, and he had been involved in politics since the 1930s, most notably as Neville Chamberlain's Parliamentary Private Secretary during the Munich crisis. On the other hand he was a skilful party manager, most of his colleagues genuinely liked him, he was popular in the country and he had a strong sense of political obligation, something much rarer nowadays.

For a time there was some debate as to whether the government should call a General Election in June or October 1964. The main disadvantage of the later date was that unofficial campaigning would go on for such a long time that people would become bored. On the other hand Labour might peak too early. A June election might mean that the electorate were still apprehensive about a Labour government, but conversely they would have the Conservatives' problems fresh in their minds. Signals at the beginning of 1964 settled the matter. The government was trailing Labour by 38% to 48%; 48% believed that Labour was more united than the Conservatives: and elections for the newly-formed Greater London Council saw swings to Labour of 6%-10%. On 9 April. Douglas-Home announced that there would be no General Election before the autumn.

In his autobiography *NAB 1*, Sir Gerald Nabarro said that Douglas-Home did not lose the 1964 election for the Conservatives, he nearly won it. Opinion polls during the late summer showed a steady fall in Labour's lead (Figure 3.1) and by early September polls were showing that a majority expected the government to win. There are several possible reasons: the government was seen as having recovered from the worst of the problems; foreign affairs, where Douglas-Home was at his most effective, were dominant; and industrial disputes harmed Labour, who were finding difficulty in sustaining the momentum of the previous two years. Thus the Conservatives felt rather happier, and it was announced on 15 September, heralded by the launch of a new newspaper, that Parliament would be dissolved ten days later, with polling day on 15 October.

The campaign

The delay in announcing the date of the General Election had given all the parties time to prepare, and the polls had them roughly level. The Conservatives fought their campaign on similar lines to 1959, mainly because their advertising agents did not know what else to do, and because the government could

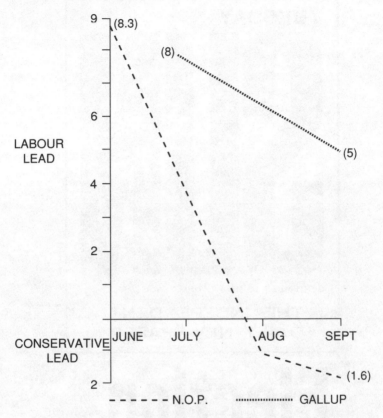

Figure 3.1 Opinion polls, June-September 1964

only campaign on their record. They did their best to stress their economic progress in their manifesto, "Prosperity with a Purpose", and towards the end Reginald Maudling made some telling points in costing Labour's programme. They presented themselves as a team, and the verdict of the writers of *The British General Election of 1964* is that they avoided any obvious disasters, and did their best with limited resources. The occasional eruption from Quintin Hogg, as when he described anyone who voted Labour as "stark, staring bonkers" (a term with a rather

Election race is on

more innocent meaning in the 1960s) did little damage, and provided much-needed excitement. In the early stages of the campaign the strategy looked to be working, when an opinion poll put the Conservatives nearly 3% ahead (30 September).

Labour's campaign focused almost completely on Harold Wilson, and he took the party's daily press conference wherever he was. To a certain extent there was a new and more professional approach, summed up in the title of their manifesto, "The New Britain". Yet Wilson seems to have gone out of his way to avoid taking professional advice during the campaign, and he determined the main issues, which was odd for someone so technologically aware. As a result there was a wide range of themes but little co-ordination, particularly with other senior members of the party. When Wilson left London to campaign in his own constituency (Huyton, in Liverpool), it was largely left to the *Daily Mirror* to sustain the momentum.

The Liberals had seen their support decline since the heady days of the Orpington success, and they failed to win the three by-elections between June 1962 and March 1963. Even so they set out to keep their organisation ready, contesting local elections and building on this to provide a basis for national success. As a result they had seen their membership double and their income treble, enabling them to double their number of full-time agents, though many were young and inexperienced, and field 365 candidates, 146 more than in 1959. Their problems were the traditional ones: too many key figures were anchored to their constituencies by small majorities; they had to keep their committed votes and win new ones; and they had to rely to a greater extent on news coverage for television exposure before the campaign officially began. Once polling day had been announced they were able to distance themselves from the bickering of the two major parties and to set themselves a target of 3 million votes. This was helped by gaining 3 election broadcasts to the 5 for the other parties, compared with the 4.4.1 ratio of 1959. Apparently those 3 broadcasts cost a total of £320.

The role of television had increased generally, so that once again 1964 was termed the "television election": 90% of homes now possessed a set, 20% higher than 1959. There were still disputes as to whether candidates could legally appear on television or radio, but most significant was the caution with which the election was treated compared with what has been common in the 1980s and 1990s. The first of television's satire programmes "That was the Week that Was" was dropped at the end of 1963, along with anything which might possibly influence voters, and most of the analytical programmes avoided political topics. The image of political activity was largely provided by news coverage and the party election broadcasts.

Another factor to have changed concerned the opinion polls. Until 1961 Gallup had the field to themselves, but for this election they were joined by National Opinion Polls. They were broadly agreed on the state of the parties until June 1963, but then diverged on the Conservative share of the vote. In addition the parties were making more use of private polls. Labour had been using their own polls since 1956: the Conservatives had employed local polls since 1958, but only began to poll regularly after the 1959 General Election.

In its early stages this was a tired election, with the major parties largely ignoring each other's challenges, and the same issues as in 1959. This changed on the same day as the opinion poll already mentioned. On 30 September the trade figures revealed a trade deficit of £73 million for the second quarter of 1964 and a need for increased borrowing. Wilson accused the Prime Minister and the government of deceiving the public, and George Brown described the situation as the biggest economic crisis since the war. Gallup polls on 4 October showed a Labour lead of 6.5%, and three days later NOP, who consistently showed a bigger share of the vote for the Conservatives, indicated that their lead had fallen from nearly 3% to less than 1% in a week. The bookmakers' odds were 3–1 on a Labour victory at this point. Wilson's confidence visibly grew as the polls continued to show Labour comfortably ahead, and by polling day they led the Conservatives by more than 3%.

The result

Polling day, 15 October was the wettest day for weeks, which may have helped the turnout to fall for the third election running, down to 77.1%. The weather was worst in the mid-evening, a time when Labour supporters traditionally vote, and this may help to explain why the result turned out to be close. As the results came in, predictions of Labour's lead shrank, and eventually they were probably relieved to achieve a small majority. The final figures were Labour 317 (44.1% of the vote); Conservatives 304 (43.4%); Liberals 9 (11.2%) giving an overall majority of only 4. Neither of the nationalist parties achieved any success in terms of seats, but the Scottish National Party secured an average of 10.7% of the vote in the 15 seats they fought, with a massive 31.7% in West Lothian, and Plaid Cymru gained 8.4% on average, though in the 7 seats with a Welsh-speaking majority their share rose to 11.8%. Nor was there any success for any of the remaining candidates, even though the total number, 1,757, was the highest apart from 1929 and 1950. Though there were fewer women candidates from the major parties, the proportion of success was higher: for Labour 17 women won out of 33 candidates, and for the Conservatives 11 from 23.

For the Conservatives in general it was undeniably a bad result. They lost 6% of their vote in comparison with 1959, the worst loss for any party since 1945. For the first (and so far the last) time in peacetime since 1906 a Conservative government had been replaced by a non-Conservative government with a majority. The Liberals had almost doubled their share of the vote and had gained 3 seats compared with 1959, coming second in a further 54 seats, but lost 2 to Labour. Labour's share of the vote was slightly up at 44.1%, but this was the lowest share for any government since 1922, and 11,000 less than their losing share in 1959. Labour had other reasons for disappointment. They had hoped that the Liberals would do better, and so take more seats from the Conservatives. Labour also lost 5 seats to the Conservatives, but what mattered most was the nature of the loss in three cases. In Eton and Slough, Perry Barr and Smethwick there were allegations that race and immigration had been exploited by the winning candidates. Immigration from the West Indies, India and Pakistan had become a controversial issue with the passage in 1962 of the Commonwealth Immigrants Act imposing quotas, which Labour had pledged to repeal. To add to Labour's anger, in losing Smethwick they had lost Patrick Gordon Walker, who was Wilson's choice as Foreign Secretary and one of the few Labour politicians with significant experience apart from Wilson himself.

What happened?

It is much easier to explain why Labour won than it is to show why their ultimate winning margin was so small. In March 1962 Macmillan confided to his diary that "the chief difficulty at the next General Election will be the cry 'Time for a Change!'": within a year the cry had become almost general. In the first place the Conservatives had done very little to develop new ideas after the victory in 1959, assuming that the factors which had kept them in office thus far would continue to operate to their advantage. The new issues which they had risked had either proved unattractive to the electorate or unsuccessful: both, in the case of the Common Market.

This might not have been fatal if the style of the government had soon come to seem out of date. Partly this was an example of the "generation gap". Half the electorate had come on the register since 1951, 10% since 1959. The proportion of MPs who had been in the House for ten years was less than half, and under 10% had entered before 1945, and many of the new Conservatives after 1959 were restless. In *The Anatomy of Britain* Anthony Sampson referred to "a loss of dynamic and progress and a general bewilderment". In addition the early 1960s saw the arrival of satire, in the form of the revue "Beyond the Fringe", *Private Eye*, "That Was the Week that Was" and the Establishment Club: indeed the term "the Establishment" as a definition dates from this time. Macmillan was a particularly easy target, since his style amounted to self-parody at times: his offhand dismissal of the resignation of his entire treasury team as "a little local difficulty" was by no means the only example. The confidence implied by the phrase "You've never had it so good" (not what he said, in fact) could easily sound like complacency.

All this was in sharp contrast to the approach which Harold Wilson brought to opposition from the beginning of 1963. His background was very different from the leaders of the Conservative party, though Macmillan commented that if Wilson ever went to school without boots it was because he was too big for them. He had achieved great success very young: he was not yet thirty when he entered Parliament in 1945, achieved office within weeks and in 1947 became the youngest Cabinet minister since 1806. He had survived resignation in 1950, and had shaken off the influence of Bevan to achieve a substantial victory in the leadership election to replace Gaitskell.

Soon after his election to the leadership Wilson was being described as "the British Kennedy", and his recent biography spells out his admiration for the American President: "it was a revolution; it was a full-time active Presidency ... And the contrast between the sharpness of the Administration in the high command of government and what has happened in this country with Macmillan and Douglas-Home, I think it is one of the really important contrasts of our time." He developed this in the run-up to the election: for example at a Labour rally at Wembley on 12 September 1964 he said that "the choice we offer ... is between standing still, clinging to the tired philosophy of a day that is gone, or moving forward in partnership and unity to a just society, to a dynamic, expanding, confident and, above all, purposive new Britain". Even committed Tories were conceding that a Labour government was not only possible, it might be necessary.

To a certain extent this is reflected in the voting figures. The figures for support by age showed Labour well ahead among the younger age-groups, scoring well over 48% for those between 21 and 44, against well under 40% for the Tories. The figures were similar for support among male voters. Preference by social class showed a less encouraging picture, however. Labour had only 8.9% of AB voters and 24.8 of C1, less than when they lost in 1970, suggesting that middle-class voters were not altogether convinced that a Labour government would solve the problems. As in subsequent elections, the most significant issue was the cost of living, cited by 72%: no other issue was seen as most important by more than 29%, and in spite of Labour's emphasis on Conservative failures in the economy, the Tories were still ahead by 47% to 34% on the ability to handle the economy well in spite of comments by senior politicians such as Attlee that the Conservatives were all for profit while Labour existed to serve the community.

There were other factors behind Labour's small majority apart from uncertainty in the minds of the electorate. Swings varied considerably from one region to another, with the West Midlands showing a swing of 5% to the Conservatives. The register was substantially out of date, with the possible maximum turnout of under 94% of those registered. The postal vote, introduced by Labour in 1948, always worked against them, with a probable 2:1 split in favour of the Conservatives. It cost Labour a reasonable majority in 1950 as well as 1964 and contributed to the Conservative victory in 1951. Whatever the reason for the narrow margin of victory, Labour's majority was not enough for them to carry out a full programme, and left no leeway for by-election losses, as they were soon to find.

4

The General Election of 1966

Background

Attlee, who had campaigned vigorously for a Labour victory in 1964, gave the new government eighteen months: Wilson had talked of the need for "a hundred days of dynamic action" following the precedent set by Kennedy in 1961. Looking back, the authors of *The British General Election of 1966* said that there were times in 1965 when it looked as though the government could fall within a few weeks. Certainly one dominating feature was the small majority, for which Labour had not really planned, and which got worse after January 1965: it meant that Labour had to be ready for a further General Election at any time while at the same time attempting to deal with major problems, implement as many of their election pledges as they could and establish themselves as a reliable government which deserved a second chance whenever it came.

Wilson dealt deftly with the problems raised by creating a Cabinet after 13 years in opposition: one of his aides, George Wigg, calculated that there were 6 who had supported Wilson himself in the 1963 leadership election, 7 who had supported George Brown and 8 Jim Callaghan. These last two, Wilson's principal rivals for the leadership after 1963 as well as before were placed in opposition to each other, Callaghan at the Treasury, Brown heading the newly-created Department of Economic Affairs. The economy was the other dominating

feature of this parliament. On 18 October Labour learned of an
£800 million deficit on the balance of payments, which created
an immediate crisis of confidence. They decided against devaluation, largely for political reasons, though economically it was
almost certainly the only realistic option: in 1970 Brian Lapping
described all the economic measures before devaluation (which
finally came in November 1967, after the General Election) as
a waste of time. A special budget on 11 November did little to
restore confidence, and a fortnight later the government had to
take out large foreign loans. A more hopeful sign was the
Declaration of Intent on Wages, Prices and Productivity signed
on 16 December, and at the end of 1964 Labour were in a
favourable position in the polls, with the Conservatives still
blamed for the economic situation.

"Your father's not only changed his mind about Mr. Wilson, he's been
getting on at me all morning for voting Conservative."
© Express Newspapers plc

This changed at the beginning of 1965. On 21 January the Foreign Secretary, Patrick Gordon Walker, lost a by-election at Leyton with a swing of 8.7% against the government, and Frank Cousins saw Labour's majority severely cut at Nuneaton. As well as protest about the financial measures it is likely that local party workers and voters did not like being mucked about in the interests of the national party. Within the party there was opposition to the Prices and Incomes policy, and complaints about delays in bringing forward domestic legislation. Most serious was a rebellion over steel nationalisation which led to its omission from the 1965 Queen's Speech. There were swings to the Conservatives in two further by-elections, and in the May 1965 local elections Labour lost 300–400 seats with a swing against them of 6%. Understandably, Labour morale fell, and at a "council of war" a few days after the Leyton set-back it was decided that the government should now behave 'in every exercise as though a spring Election was inevitable' (Barbara Castle).

For the next few months Labour marked time, while attention shifted to the other parties. The Liberal leader Jo Grimond raised the possiblity of a coalition or at least a pact, an attractive option to a government with a majority of one. This was never particularly realistic, since neither leader could deliver the whole membership, and Wilson had no intention of conceding ground on any significant point. The Conservatives, meanwhile, had introduced a new process for choosing a leader in February, to avoid the problems encountered in 1963, and Sir Alec Douglas-Home's position was becoming steadily less secure. The campaign to replace him grew in strength from April, with every criticism leaving him a little weaker, until he finally resigned on 22 July. The election of a new leader proceeded smoothly, though the choice of Edward Heath was a little surprising to a general public which apparently favoured Reginald Maudling. In August Heath's approval rating was 51%, above Wilson's for the only time in the parliament, compared with Douglas-Home's 32% only a month before.

For some reason Labour's position in the polls recovered in

September 1965, and the mood of panic never returned. Wilson's ratings were as high as Eden or Macmillan at their peak, and the Conservatives rapidly fell back. Partly this reflected growing stability in the economy, with the announcement of the National Plan and a steady pound. Another reason was the serious difficulties in which the Conservatives found themselves over Rhodesia (now Zimbabwe). The white minority government of Ian Smith had been threatening to break away for some time, and in November 1965 had finally issued a Unilateral Declaration of Independence. During the earlier months of 1965 Wilson had been negotiating to prevent this, but once it had happened it created more problems for the opposition. Heath supported the government line, and in the crucial debate on 21 December advised his party to abstain, but 50 voted against the government and a further 31 with Labour.

Labour's recovery meant that Wilson could choose the date of the General Election rather than having it forced upon him. He had announced in June 1965 that there would be no election before 1966, and for a time seems to have favoured waiting until October, as some of the Cabinet advised. Certainly this is what the Conservatives were expecting, and hoping for. The clinching factor seems to have been the by-election in Hull North at the end of January. The Conservatives needed a swing of only 1% to take the seat, but Labour's Kevin Macnamara not only held it, the swing of 4.5% to Labour was the biggest to a government in a marginal seat since 1924. Since Labour had been well ahead in the polls for four months and Wilson enjoyed a 20% lead over Heath there was no longer any need to delay, especially if there were going to be further problems in the autumn. Wilson therefore announced on 28 February that Parliament would rise on 10 March, allowing time for Callaghan to introduce a "mini-budget", and that polling day would be three weeks later, on 31 March. This had the added advantage that there would be a virtually new register of electors, which ought to increase Labour's chances of gaining the lead they needed and expected.

The campaign

In her diaries Barbara Castle described the 1966 election campaign as "one of the most boring . . . I have ever experienced . . . there was an air of unreality. I felt the campaign was merely an unavoidable hiatus in our work, and I think this is what the country felt". George Brown, who carried out the same sort of speaking tour as in 1970 (and which Richard Crossman dismissed as already old-fashioned) only mentioned the 1966 election in passing. The *Daily Mail* complained that every issue had already been canvassed and discussed to the point of tedium, and the chapter in *The British General Election of 1966* mainly deals with what did not happen, and issues that failed to emerge. It is a sign of the lack of real incident during the campaign that a great deal of attention was devoted to largely futile shadow-boxing over debates between the leaders on television: as usual, they failed to happen. The Conservatives and the newspapers tried to generate interest in allegations of intimidation and "kangaroo courts" by some unions, but this died out after the first week.

The Conservative manifesto "Action, not Words", based on the earlier policy document "Putting Britain Right Ahead" was better received than that of Labour. Since 1964 the Conservatives had been reforming their organisation and their policies. The new Party Chairman, Edward du Cann, was only forty, nine years younger than his leader; there was to be greater focus on business ideas and techniques, and a general streamlining of Central Office; and there was to be a campaign of fund-raising, since the party had spent virtually everything in trying to avoid defeat in 1964. In policy terms they focused on five main areas: the economy, Europe, trade union reform, social services and housing, determined partly by survey evidence as to what key groups of voters saw as most significant, partly by what was ready when the election was called. Unfortunately there was little co-ordination between Heath's meticulously-planned campaign and what other Conservative leaders were doing, and the choice of five policy areas to project created confusion in the minds of an electorate which was not particularly interested anyway.

Labour campaigned under the slogan "You *know* Labour Government Works". Though Wilson had to appear to be governing the country as well as campaigning, he addressed at least one meeting every day, but otherwise there was no precise planning: Richard Crossman confided to his diary that "the daily strategy meetings at Transport House have been a fraud because nothing has been happening." Labour concentrated on their slogans, avoiding getting entangled in complex arguments and making more attacks on the Tories than in 1964, since they were seeking endorsement for a further term, not to replace a discredited government. Their manifesto "Time for Decision" contained little new, and was summed up by one campaign organiser as "the last 16 months plus the next year" which may help to explain the feeling that the government ran out of ideas later in the Parliament, creating a sense of disappointment among erstwhile supporters.

The Liberals had never really sorted out their strategy during this Parliament. Their leader, Jo Grimond, was hostile to the Conservatives but disillusioned with Labour, and never got to grips with the implications of the suggestion that there might be a deal with the government. Though they had an early success when David Steel won Roxburgh from the Tories, morale and support slumped, and in two of the three by-elections held in the winter of 1965–1966 their share of the vote dropped by more than half. They fielded 311 candidates in 1966, 54 less than in 1964, but more than looked likely at one time. Their main claim was that they could act as a brake on Labour ambitions: the polls offered no hope that they might hold the balance.

Television continued to increase in importance, with around 10% of each evening's viewing on BBC1 being devoted to politics. The parties had succeeeded in keeping the 5:5:3 split in broadcasts, though the overall time was reduced. Some complained that there was too much politics, and that 15-minute broadcasts were too long, but this was not confirmed by the audience figures: on the other hand a survey on 7 April. showed that two-thirds would not mind if there were no party political broadcasts. Surveys on the image of the leaders on television confirmed the general trends. Wilson was seen as the most impressive by 49%, against 19% for Heath and 12% for Grimond. Significantly 27% of Conservative voters found Wilson the most effective, whereas only 5% of Labour voters were attracted by Heath.

The result

The turnout was the lowest post-war at 75.8%, though 42% claimed to be very interested in the campaign, compared with 36% at the same stage in 1964. The main fall was in safe Labour seats, and super-marginals showed an average turnout of over 81%. Labour had largely maintained their poll lead over the Conservatives, slipping slightly from 15.5% on 19 March to 13.5% on 25 March, and Wilson had remained well ahead of Heath. The winning margin was not so great, for reasons which have become more apparent in the 1980s and 1990s, that the polls have tended to overestimate Labour support, as discussed in a later chapter, though only the polls published by the *Daily Express* were wildly out. Even so the Labour vote was up by 750,000 and the Conservatives down by over 500,000 compared with 1964, giving a winning margin (47.9% to 41.9%) which was the largest since 1945, though it has since been bettered by the margins of Conservative victory in 1979, 1983 and 1987. The Conservative share of the vote was their lowest since 1945, and the overall result was virtually a mirror image of 1959, with Labour having 363 seats and the Conservatives 253. The Liberal result was rather odd: though their share of the vote had fallen to 8.5% they had managed to hold 12 seats, three more than in 1964. Much of this was by the skin of their teeth, since in 10 of their seats they had majorities of less than 2,500, and they lost ground in most of the seats they fought in 1964 and 1966.

The swing was remarkably uniform across the country, deviating little from the UK average of 3.1%, though it was barely 2% in Scotland on the one hand and 3.9% in the West Midlands (6% in Birmingham) on the other. This is confirmed by the number of seats changing hands: it is estimated that if the swing had been *totally* uniform between 1959 and 1966 Labour would have won 100 seats from the Tories, when in fact they won 103. There was no evidence of tactical voting. Richard Crossman described the result as "a presidential victory of extraordinary proportions", and there was no doubt that Wilson had gained the convincing mandate he had sought.

What happened?

Barbara Castle's verdict was that the electorate "had made up their minds at the start and they remained unchanged." There is no reason to quarrel with this as the government had largely avoided making serious mistakes since 1964 and had done enough to convince the electorate that they deserved to continue. By contrast the Conservatives had not had time to recover from the problems of their last period in government, though they reckoned that they could have done much better with another nine months to prepare. Heath had made little impact, though his last television broadcast had attracted some approval: he was seen as cold and remote, and by February 1966 his rating was below that of Douglas-Home. The Conservatives were still being blamed for the economic difficulties, 42% blaming them as against 16% blaming Labour. There had been little time for the new policies to get through to the party, let alone the electorate, and many in the party conceded that they were preparing to win the *next* election rather than 1966.

Richard Crossman's assessment is more open to argument. In his view, "The middle classes really want(ed) us to win . . . Harold's personality has been a great help – middle class, not professional or upper class . . . They recognise in him a man of their own kind whom they are proud to have at No. 10; they feel they have a competent government and will vote for it". No one would disagree with his verdicts on the importance of Wilson's reputation or the perceived competence of the government, but there has to be some doubt about his opinions on class support. Certainly Labour had nearly doubled their vote among AB voters by comparison with 1964 (15.5% as against 8.9%) and increased their C1 vote significantly (24.8% in 1964, 29.9% in 1966). Yet their C1 vote was to be higher in the *losing* year of 1970 (and in 1992), and their most significant share of the vote came in C2 (58.5% in 1966 compared with 54.4% in 1964) and DE (65.2% compared with 59.1%): indeed Labour has never again had this level of support among working class voters, nor the Conservatives so little.

Even so, the possibility that voters were swinging generally to Labour, with particularly large swings among the 25–34 and over 65 age-groups raises the question as to whether the two General Elections of the 1960s constitute a watershed. Like every General Election, the answer has to be that it was in some respects, but not in others. It did not mark a decisive shift in Labour's favour, since they were never to do so well again, and may never again come anywhere near their 1966 success. Nor did the 1964 and 1966 elections represent "a democratic *coup d'état*: a symbolic shock that altered the way the British people thought about themselves more profoundly than any other event since the Second World War" as Harold Wilson's biographer has written of 1964. This confuses cause and effect. The results of these General Elections were part of the process in which the people of Britain came to terms with changed circumstances both domestically and internationally, but they did not cause it.

In other senses these elections do represent a decisive break with the past. In terms of political leadership, since 1965 only one major party leader (Michael Foot) and no Prime Minister has come from an independent school, and the election of Edward Heath marked the beginning of the end of the aristocratic domination of the Conservative Party since the Second World War. Under Heath the Conservatives began another phase of the process of re-invention which has enabled the party to survive and adapt. In the Labour party the change was in the age and occupational background of MPs. In 1959 and 1964 the median age of Labour members was seven years older than the Conservatives: in 1966 this gap had fallen to eighteen months. After the 1964 election 52% of Labour members were from the professional and business classes, and 42% were graduates:

32% were workers. The intake of new members in 1965 and 1966 had 65% professional and business, and 68% were graduates, while the proportion of workers was only 14%. Both parties were therefore in the process of moving away from their origins and becoming more technocratic and meritocratic: to adapt their own phrases, in 1964 a 14th Earl had been replaced by a 14th Mr Wilson.

Whatever the implications for the future, there was one certain message from the General Election of 1966: there could now be no excuses for Labour. They had secured the majority they needed to continue and expand their programme, and seemed to be more in tune with the prevailing mood than an opposition which was in the process of coming to terms with that mood. Anything which went wrong for the government henceforth would be their own fault.

5
The General Election of 1970

Background

When Harold Wilson called the General Election in 1966 it was with the intention of increasing a majority which by then had almost disappeared. With a swing from Conservative to Labour of 3.5% his hopes were amply fulfilled, and with an overall majority of ninety-six he had the secure base for a legislative programme that he had not achieved in 1964.

From some points of view the Labour government from 1966 to 1970 could be seen as a success. In the economic field the government largely survived the set-back of devaluation in November 1967 when the dollar/pound parity was cut from $2.80 to $2.40. There was admittedly some criticism of Wilson's claim that "the pound in your pocket has not been devalued", and Iain Macleod, the Conservatives' economics spokesman had enjoyed himself at the Party Conference by pointing out that "there have been three Labour Prime Ministers; Mr. Ramsay MacDonald, Lord Attlee and Wilson: and they have all devalued the pound", and that "Mr. Callaghan has one great defect as a Chancellor: he's always wrong. For Jim Callaghan the laws of averages have been suspended." On the whole, however, the Conservatives had not made much capital out of any of the economic issues. Most of the criticism of the decision to devalue was that it had been delayed too long. The pound was clearly overvalued against the dollar and the West German mark, and all the various economic initiatives before 1967 had been a waste of time, based on political rather than economic considerations. It was his record on the economy that led to Harold Wilson being dubbed "the best Conservative Prime Minister around", not least because the Conservatives apparently had nothing else to suggest.

Another area of success for the Labour government was in the field of social legislation, especially the work of Roy Jenkins as Home Secretary from December 1965 until he replaced Callaghan at the Exchequer: the Race Relations Act of 1968 was widely seen not only as a major personal achievement but as one of the most significant acts of the entire government. This had provoked a vigorous response from Duncan Sandys and especially from Enoch Powell, but their line was immediately repudiated by the Conservative leadership, and Powell was sacked from the Shadow Cabinet, demonstrating that opposition policy was not significantly different from that of the government.

The issue of industrial relations did cause serious difficulties for the government for much of 1969. Wilson became convinced that some recent strikes, such as the dockers', had been politically motivated and aimed at damaging the United Kingdom's economic recovery. He therefore gave Barbara Castle a virtually free hand to devise legislation to prevent damaging strikes, in spite of the evidence from the Donovan Commission among others that such legislation was not likely to work. The result was a White Paper "In Place of Strife", which proposed, among other things, ballots of union members before strike action, and a compulsory "cooling-off period" before a strike call could be implemented. Understandably these proposals caused immense disagreement within the Labour Party at all levels, particularly in the Cabinet, where Wilson and Castle were the only strong enthusiasts for the proposals. Wilson's determination to press on was emphasised by the abandonment of a bill to reform the House of Lords, which had been a manifesto commitment, and with which the government had been toying since 1964. The revolt against them seems to have been led by Callaghan, who made it clear that not only could he not personally support a bill based on "In Place of Strife", but as Party Treasurer he could not guarantee that enough money would be provided by the unions for a future General Election campaign if the bill became law. In addition the Chief Whip was afraid of a major rebellion within the Parliamentary Party if a bill came before the House of Commons: party discipline was a serious problem throughout this administration, since with so large a majority, dissident Labour members assumed they could rebel whenever they liked. The upshot was that "In Place of Strife" was dropped in return for a "Solemn and Binding Undertaking" from the unions to avoid strikes which might be damaging to the government or the economy.

There is little doubt that there was considerable short-term damage to the government from this episode. One minister complained that as usual, not enough work had been done on it, so that the government had made itself look amateur, silly and childish, and Labour's rating in the opinion polls slumped, though it is not easy to know which did the more harm, the initial proposals or the decision to drop them. Either way, it looked as though no long-term harm had been done, since by May 1970 Labour had recovered to register a 7% lead over the Conservatives, who once again had not been able to make much capital out of the issue.

During the intervening years it has become clear that for many people this apparent success did not outweigh their feelings of growing disappointment as the Labour government went on. Part of this was a general feeling that much more could have been done to transform and liberalise society, particularly after the "thirteen years of Tory misrule" from 1951 to 1964, and that after 1968 the government seemed to have run out of ideas. People could still look back to the previous Labour government 1945–1951, which had created the Welfare State and the National Health Service, as well as nationalising many key industries, and wonder why nothing comparable had happened since 1966. There had, for example, been no new nationalisations (a term which Wilson never used, preferring to talk of "public ownership").

As well as the things the Labour government had not done, many of its actions were disliked, not least by the left wing of the party. The decision to support American bombing campaigns in Vietnam, the 1968 Commonwealth Immigrants Act, which sought to limit immigration in the wake of the expulsion of Asians from Kenya and the cuts in health and housing programmes, added to the industrial relations proposals were strongly criticised at the time and have been attacked by a new generation of writers during the last few years.

In all probability the Cabinet was unaware of these feelings by the beginning of 1970: the main thing on their minds was the timing of the next General Election, and the sort of budget which ought to precede it. Certainly Wilson had no intention of allowing himself to be pushed close to the five-year limit as Douglas-Home had been in 1964, and the general expectation was that he would call the election in October 1970. Many of the Cabinet favoured this, coupled with a high-risk budget, and as late as April Richard Crossman was describing June as clearly impossible. Many of Labour's traditional supporters would be on holiday, and many would probably not bother to return home to vote: an additional complication was that the England football team would be defending the World Cup which they had won in 1966, and football in Mexico was likely to attract far more interest than an election campaign.

It is not easy to assess what made Wilson change his mind. The budget introduced by Roy Jenkins was certainly not the "high-risk" exercise favoured by Crossman and others, indeed there was some disappointment that it had not done more, and a feeling that it could have been much more adventurous without jeopardising the economy. Possibly Wilson felt that the government's record was enough, particularly in view of the lack of really vigorous opposition from the Conservatives; possibly he was afraid that if he waited until October there might be problems which would undermine the chances of a third victory. Certainly 18 June was seen by his colleagues as Wilson's choice. Some people grumbled that he had made up his mind some time before and then waited for events to justify his decision; and that the United Kingdom was moving once again in the direction of Prime Ministerial Elections.

The campaign

For a number of reasons the 1970 election campaign was fairly unexciting. In the first place a month was probably too long to sustain interest, particularly during the summer and with the distractions of the World Cup and its attendant excitements such as the arrest of the England captain for theft. Wilson and Heath had been the opponents in 1966, and their styles were fairly well known, as was the main thrust of their campaign strategies, with the government stressing its achievements, and the Conservatives finding it difficult, at least in the early stages, to put forward a convincing alternative or to find new issues. In the same way the conduct of the campaigns showed Labour as apparently the better organised, with the Conservatives stumbling along behind, without many ideas of their own and self-consciously borrowing from Labour.

In spite of all this, there are several interesting features in this campaign. There was far greater concentration on the leaders themselves, particularly at the daily news conferences: this led to the description of the campaign as an "unpopularity contest" in "The British General Election of 1970". Very few politicians made a national impact apart from Wilson and Heath, though George Brown addressed ninety-eight meetings in a fortnight for Labour. Enoch Powell made some impact towards the end of the campaign, particularly in the area around his own constituency in Wolverhampton, and some Labour politicians believed that there was some sympathy among their supporters for Powell's views on immigration and race relations. Nationally Powell attracted the greatest notice when Heath announced that he would not include Powell in his Cabinet, though there is no means of knowing what impact this might have had on the result.

The concentration on the leaders was further emphasised by the lack of impact of third parties, especially the Liberals. Though Jo Grimond had been replaced as leader in 1967 by the

younger Jeremy Thorpe, they had made no real headway in
picking up votes since 1964, and during the campaign Thorpe
attracted less attention than Powell. They were very short of
funds, and were able to field candidates in only 332 of the 630
constituencies.

The media played a much greater role in the campaign than
previously: the news conferences were geared to radio and
television as much as to the newspapers, and there were "phone-
in" programmes with all the party leaders. The most novel
feature was the enormous number of opinion polls and the
attention they attracted. New polls appeared virtually every day,
and they showed wide variations: on 13 June one poll gave
Labour a lead of 12.5% over the Conservatives, while another
on the following day showed the lead down to 2.5%. One thing
on which they were virtually all agreed as polling day approached
was that Labour should win comfortably, probably with a
majority of between fifty and seventy, which compared very
favourably with their majority of sixty-six at the dissolution.
Certainly Wilson was speculating on what could be offered to
"poor old Ted" (Heath) when he lost again. Some cynics have
also suggested that Powell was also expecting a Labour victory in
spite of his advice on 16 June to "Vote and vote Tory", and his
expressed intention of taking attention from Labour by his
speeches late in the campaign. If Heath lost, the way would be
open for Powell to make a bid for the leadership he had failed to
gain in 1965.

The result

Polling day was a beautiful day across the country, something
which traditionally was supposed to favour Labour. They also
expected to gain from the postponement of boundary changes,
which usually mean an increase in potential Conservative seats,
as explained in Chapter 1, and possibly from the widening of the
franchise in 1969. This gave the vote to people over eighteen and
removed that curious anomaly known as the "Y" voter, which
meant that people who reached voting age while a register was in

operation (February to February) could not vote until the new register came into force. From 1969 people could vote the moment they reached eighteen.

This increase in the potential electorate may help to explain why the turnout was the lowest in percentage terms since 1935 at 72%, since the actual *number* of voters was up by over a million, though many attempts were made to use the turnout as an explanation for the result.

The only indication that the opinion polls had got it wrong was a poll conducted by Opinion Research Centre on polling day itself which showed a tiny Conservative lead, but even this did not prepare politicians or observers for what actually happened: as politicians repeatedly say in the face of adverse poll findings, the poll that matters is the one on the day itself. The first result at Guildford showed a swing of 4.4% to the Conservatives: the third, Stanley Orme's seat in Salford showed a much greater swing, and according to his own account, this is the point at which Harold Wilson became seriously worried. In fact the early results showed the greatest swings, with both Wolverhampton seats showing swings of about 9%, and the highest being in Cannock, where Jenny Lee, Aneurin Bevan's widow lost after a swing against her of nearly 11%.

This swing produced the most memorable image of the entire campaign. One of the features of the BBC coverage of elections during the 1960s and 1970s was the "Swingometer" which showed the gains and losses in seats between the major parties according to the swing indicated by the results. No-one had expected much of a swing to the Conservatives, let alone 9% or 10%, and so in the early hours of the morning a technician appeared with a pot of paint and a brush to extend the scale.

The Conservatives gained an overall majority at about 5 a.m., and the final result gave the Conservatives 330 (46.4% of the vote): Labour 288 (43.0%): Liberals 6 (7.5%), an overall majority of 30. In fact this is the last time (at the time of writing) that an overall majority for one party was converted into an overall majority for the other. There were 6 others elected, 1 Scottish Nationalist, 1 other in England and 4 in Northern

Ireland. The average swing over the country was 4.8%, a post-war record. It was remarkably uniform, within about 2% either way within the major regions. Some areas did show a greater deviation: the average for the 18 Merseyside seats was 2.5%, and rural Wales, Tyneside and most of Scotland showed lower than average swings; of the high swings the Oldham/Bolton area showed 7.4%, and the Black Country and Leicester were also high.

The number of seats changing hands was also a record (88) and the Conservatives made a record number of gains (66). There were several notable casualties on the Labour front bench. As well as Jenny Lee (Arts Minister), George Brown, Foreign Secretary until 1968, lost Belper, partly as a result of the amount of time he spent on his national campaign, and partly through a great deal of new building in his constituency which housed mainly Conservative owner-occupiers. Labour did at least regain 9 of the 15 seats they had lost in by-elections, but there was considerable embarrassment caused by the poor showing by black candidates, especially the swing of 10.8% against David Pitt in Clapham, a seat he was expected to hold fairly easily. The Liberals lost 7 seats, and in some others their majority was reduced to a few hundred, so that it was scant consolation that their vote per candidate was as high as in 1955. The nationalist parties received something of a set-back, in that the Scottish Nationalists lost Hamilton, but won the Western Isles, while Plaid Cymru lost Carmarthen, which they had won in 1966. There was very little evidence that either of the nationalist parties was anything other than a refuge for protest between General Elections.

What happened?

Understandably most of the debate centred on why Labour lost an election they were apparently going to win comfortably. One set of explanations, given currency by Richard Crossman, among others, focussed on timing. The first suggestion was that Wilson had forced a reluctant Cabinet and party into a June election when common sense was pointing to October. Wilson clearly did not believe this, indeed he thought that a small and reasonably secure majority in June, which the opinion polls and local government results were indicating, was preferable to a possibly larger, but more risky majority in October. We shall never know whether an October election would have given the government time to get over the problems which led to them losing in June, but on all the available evidence it is difficult to support this explanation.

It is easier to believe that the campaign was a week too long. This has nothing to do with possible boredom; quite simply, the major set-backs for the government came during the last few days of the campaign, and if polling day had been 11 June rather than the 18th it is possible that Labour might have won.

Another set of reasons concerned the opinion polls, which were believed in several quarters to have given a totally misleading picture throughout the campaign. This view was particularly popular with Conservatives, who claimed that they were never behind. It is true that there may well have been a large body of *potential* Conservative voters who made up their minds very late, but it is very unlikely that all the polls could have made major sampling or interviewing errors, or suffered from what has since been termed "tactical lying" even with the comparatively unsophisticated techniques in use at the time. The only plausible impact of the polls over the whole campaign may have been to induce a certain amount of complacency among Labour voters; the feeling that since the polls showed Labour likely to win easily there was no need for them actually to go and vote. Something similar may have happened in 1966 and in October 1974, when Labour also won fewer votes than the polls were suggesting.

The aspect of the opinion polls which does seem to be beyond question is that most of them stopped questioning too early, and so missed a very late swing from Labour to Conservative. This explanation merely raises other questions, however: why did so many people decide to vote Conservative rather than vote Labour or abstain? To what extent can the result be explained by disillusioned Labour voters staying at home? Certainly this last view represents the current Labour orthodoxy of authors such as Ken Livingstone and Clive Ponting, and probably starts with Crossman, who detected a great deal of resentment at broken promises both locally in his Coventry constituency, and nationally. This is borne out by the very hostile questioning which Wilson encountered on the BBC's "Election Forum", far more severe than that directed at the other leaders. On the other hand the evidence does not really support the claim of massive abstentions among Labour voters, indeed the greatest fall in turnout was in the south-east, not in traditional Labour areas.

Far more plausible is the belief that events in the last week of the campaign confirmed the decision of a great many waverers to vote Conservative. Possibly Powell's intervention, and England's loss to West Germany in the World Cup had a marginal effect, but the main factor was the economy, and more precisely, the belief that Conservative warnings were right. On 1 June Lord Cromer, a former Governor of the Bank of England warned that the incoming government would face a more difficult financial situation than in 1964. The polls were suggesting that a majority would prefer a Conservative government if there were an economic crisis, but Conservative forecasts of gloom and "sham sunshine" looked increasingly hollow when a trade deficit of £59 million in April had fallen to £14 million in May and was expected to fall further. Instead the figures announced on 15 June, the Monday before polling day showed an increased deficit of £31 million, and suggested that Labour had been unduly complacent about economic prospects.

It is one thing for a voter to decide that he is unhappy with the party he has hitherto supported, but it is quite another to decide to vote for another party. There were in fact several signs that the Conservatives had been regaining credibility even before the trade figures were announced. Although Heath was still regarded as prickly and defensive at times, he had gained a great deal of credit for his victory in the Sydney to Hobart yacht race. The meeting of senior Conservatives at Selsdon Park had enabled Wilson to make jibes about "Selsdon Man", but had brought the Conservatives more into the public eye, and had enabled them to hammer out a clear set of policy and manifesto commitments reflecting Heath's views and style.

Equally important was the overhaul of the Conservative Party organisation after 1966. Finances had been revived by fund-raising and by making economies, the links between back-benchers and leadership and organisation and Parliament had been strengthened by the appointment of a professional deputy chairman, and the party had regularly been commissioning private opinion polls.

By contrast the Labour organisation seemed little developed from the stage when Wilson had described it as a "penny-farthing" in 1955. Wilson himself regarded a strong party organisation as more nuisance than it was worth, but there were undeniable defects which, if remedied, might have enabled Labour to hang on to seats which they narrowly lost. Relations between party headquarters, then still at Transport House, and the parliamentary leadership were often strained, and there were disagreements on policy. Money was tight: there were only 146 full-time agents, the budget for Party Political Broadcasts in 1969 was a mere £2,500 and only £200,000 was allocated to advertising. Membership had fallen to about 300,000, and active membership was lower still. Perhaps most seriously, and reinfor-cing the arguments about timing, Transport House seems to have been expecting the General Election in October 1970 and to have been caught unawares by the decision to go to the country in June, whereas Conservative Central Office was ready.

The result of the 1970 General Election is in many ways one of the most surprising since the war, if not this century. Not only did the government expect to win, most of the opposition expected them to as well. Edward Heath was almost the only person to believe that he would be the next Prime Minister.

6

The General Election of February 1974

Background

The Conservative administration which came to power so unexpectedly in June 1970 provides a very good example of the dangers of doing too much: as Gladstone, among others, found in 1874, the more the government does, the more people it annoys. Right from the start, there were policy decisions which were to have major consequences both for the timing and the outcome of the General Election, particularly in the four areas of the economy, industrial relations, the Common Market and Northern Ireland.

The kindest thing that can be said about Conservative economic policy was that it was inconsistent. Within a few weeks of the General Election there was a major set-back with the sudden death of Iain Macleod, Heath's choice as Chancellor of the Exchequer. Not only did this force a re-shuffle before the administration had really started (Macleod was replaced by Anthony Barber, who had originally been put in charge of the Common Market negotiations), it removed from the Cabinet a figure of major political stature, like Heath and Maudling a protégé of R. A. Butler immediately after the war, who might have been able to influence some of the decisions taken later on.

In line with the manifesto, the approach to the economy was initially tough, with much that would nowadays be termed "Thatcherite". There was to be tight control of the money supply and public spending to bring inflation under control, giving rise to Heath's much-misunderstood pledge to cut the rate of price rises "at a stroke", and there was to be an end to the uncontrolled bailing-out of industries which got into difficulties, what the new Industry Secretary John Davies (brought from the Confederation of British Industry (CBI) straight into the Cabinet) termed "lame ducks".

By the later part of 1971 there was a major shift in policy, dubbed by Enoch Powell and others a "U-turn", a term now used to describe even minor changes. At least it was not too wide of the mark in 1971. The "Barber boom" stressed the need for growth in the economy as more important than keeping inflation down. This was to have long-term effects, but more immediately surprising was the decision to nationalise Rolls-Royce in order to preserve vital defence contracts, not only because the Conservatives had no tradition of extending the public sector, though they had largely accepted what Labour had done between 1945 and 1951, but also because Labour appeared to have abandoned nationalisation as well, on the evidence of their 1964–1970 administration.

Another major surprise was the decision to introduce a statutory wage policy in 1972. Although earlier Conservative chancellors such as Selwyn Lloyd had done this, it had been ruled out at the beginning of the Heath administration. It began with a complete wage freeze which was followed by two complicated phases of restraint involving government-imposed norms and thresholds based on rises in the cost of living. These were intended to damp down inflationary wage demands, but had the reverse effect since what the government intended as a maximum rise was widely used as a minimum in wage bargaining.

Curbs on wages gave a new twist to the issue of industrial relations, another problem from the beginning of this administration. The Conservatives had committed themselves in their 1970 manifesto to introduce legislation regulating trade unions, and the Industrial Relations Act had become law in 1971. It had immediately run into total opposition from the unions. Though

"Very well, Prime Minister – we'll see you round here about four p.m.
then we'll all be able to explain your Phase 3 to you."
© Express Newspapers plc

much of it was in line with Labour's "In Place of Strife" there
were several specific elements that were loathed. In an attempt to
provide a judicial framework for industrial relations disputes
without bringing unions within the scope of the existing criminal
law, an Industrial Relations Court was set up with powers to fine
unions or sequestrate their funds: this led to a series of
confrontations which particularly involved the Amalgamated
Union of Engineering Workers (AUEW) and their General
Secretary Hugh Scanlon. In order to operate legally under the
Act, such as operating a closed shop, unions had to be
registered: the government hoped to avoid difficulty by deciding
that all unions would automatically be registered unless they
chose to de-register. To the dismay of the government virtually

all unions decided not to co-operate, and to oppose all aspects of the Act as vigorously as they could. In order for their wages policy to work, the government needed the co-operation of the unions if possible, certainly during the phases of restraint. In an attempt to secure this, the government tacitly dropped the Industrial Relations Act, though it remained on the statute book. By then the damage was done: the industrial relations climate had been irretrievably soured. There were particular problems with fuel and power, with power cuts evry winter from 1970, and in 1972 a miners' strike was settled by a substantial award as the result of an independent enquiry headed by Lord Wilberforce.

Edward Heath had been committed to taking the United Kingdom into the Common Market since Harold Macmillan had put him in charge of the unsuccessful negotiations in the early 1960s, but the Conservative manifesto devoted only two hundred words in a document of thirty pages to the issue, and was decidedly ambiguous on the question of consent. "Our sole commitment is to negotiate; no more, no less ... A Conservative government would not be prepared to recommend to Parliament, nor would Members of Parliament approve, a settlement which was unequal or unfair. In making this judgement, Ministers and Members will listen to the views of their constituents." Heath decided that the General Election victory and the substantial House of Commons vote in favour of the principle of entry gave him a sufficient mandate for entry, a point of view that provoked considerable disagreement. Many people wanted to see Heath's claim of "full-hearted consent" tested by some sort of consultative process such as a referendum. The United Kingdom's fellow applicants all held such a process, and Norway's application for membership was withdrawn when a majority voted against. This was suggested, unkindly, as a reason for the lack of any formal consultation in the United Kingdom. The other parties were quick to exploit these issues. Labour very soon put their recriminations at losing in 1970 behind them, and could probably not believe their luck in avoiding the honeymoon period which they had expected the government to enjoy. They committed themselves to repeal the Industrial Relations Act as soon as they came to office, and promised that there would be a re-negotiation of the terms of entry to the European Community and a referendum on the whole question. Electorally the Liberals benefited from the Conservatives' problems, as they had done in the 1960s, winning a number of traditionally Conservative seats such as Ely, Ripon and Sutton and Cheam and by September 1973 standing at 30% in opinion polls.

In spite of all these difficulties, the Conservative Party Conference in October 1973 was in optimistic mood. It was confidently expected that they would go to the country in October 1974 or later, and would reap the benefit of pursuing tough but necessary economic measures. Over the next few months this confidence was shattered. In October the Arab nations declared war on Israel (the Yom Kippur War), and though they did not have the victory they expected, they discovered that oil was a powerful political weapon against the industrialised nations, and raised prices fourfold. Though in the long term this made it profitable to extract oil from the North Sea (when oil was cheap the capital costs were prohibitive), in the short term it not only had a drastic impact on the balance of payments, it gave the miners an extremely powerful bargaining position in opposing Phase III of the government's incomes policy. In November they began an overtime ban, which led the government to declare a State of Emergency on 13 November. On 28 November the miners' leaders went to Downing Street, but the Industrial Relations Act had created a mood of suspicion already. This was heightened by poor liaison between the miners and the Department of Employment: Joe Gormley, the National Union of Mineworkers (NUM) President seems to have been the only contact, and there was very little information about the miners' possible intentions.

Though Gormley was a moderate trade unionist, in spite of the way in which he was portrayed at the time, there were others in the NUM who were more opposed to any agreement with the government, and there was a great deal of controversy and anger at remarks attributed to the Scottish NUM leader Mick

McGahey that his aim was to break the pay code and force the Conservatives out. A major problem was that stocks of coal at the power stations were low, and little was being moved from the pit-heads: the government therefore announced on 13 December that in the New Year industry would be put on a three-day week. Within the Conservative Party the feeling was growing that a settlement with the miners could not be achieved without a General Election, possibly as early as 7 February, an idea taken up in the press, though Enoch Powell condemned it as "an act of total immorality". Although a Trades Union Congress (TUC) promise not to use any settlement with the miners as a precedent in future wage bargaining was rejected by Anthony Barber and by the CBI, Heath promised to consider it, and optimism grew when fuel stocks turned out to be better than had been feared, raising the possibility of a four-day week at worst. Most of Heath's colleagues except William Whitelaw were unconvinced about the possibility of a settlement, but Heath was not prepared to confide in them: apparently the issue was never discussed in the full Cabinet. Whatever chance there might have been was shattered on 4 February 1974, when the result of a miners' ballot showed 81% in favour of a strike and against giving the government more time. On 7 February the dissolution of Parliament was announced with polling day scheduled for 28 February.

The campaign

The government had suffered most from the uncertainty: they were blamed for the general situation, and for raising expectations which had not been fulfilled. In addition the speculation about an election in early February had given the opposition parties time to get ready, though the Labour manifesto was still not complete. Overall there was a sense of relief that something concrete was going to happen, and that all the problems would be settled one way or the other. It was clearly in everybody's interests to have the shortest possible campaign.

There were two main issues: the industrial relations climate and the economy. The government naturally wanted to campaign on the first, which they depicted, in an adaptation of the "peers versus people" campaign of 1910, as "unions versus government", especially since they were well ahead in the polls on this issue. Unfortunately for them, it dropped out of the campaign during the first ten days. The railway workers agreed to Wilson's request that they should suspend any industrial action until after the election, and clearly there would be no settlement by the miners until they knew which party would form the government. The Relativities Board had been set up to arbitrate over "special cases" and to allow exceptions to the strict operation of the Phase III formulas. The government had apparently been considering the miners as a special case before the election, and the Relativities Board agreed that they deserved significantly more than the norm. Even more damage was done by figures released by the Pay Board on 21 February. One of the government's main arguments in the dispute had been that the miners were easily at the head of the earnings league, whereas the Pay Board contended that they were below the average for manual workers. This suggested that the miners' pay claim had been mishandled and that the whole crisis and election had been unnecessary. This view was supported by 52% of voters who retained a strong Conservative identification and 70% of those who abandoned their identification.

Industrial relations were seen as the main issue by only 40% of voters at the start of the campaign and 24% at the end; for the majority, the main factor was the economy. Virtually all the information released on the economy during the campaign went against the government. On 15 February price figures showed a rise of 35% in all prices and 50% in food prices: ten days later the highest ever trade deficit of £383 million was announced. Unlike 1970, however, the main opposition party did not benefit, nor were they apparently helped by Enoch Powell's advice that those who wished the United Kingdom to leave Europe should vote Labour. He had already decided that he would not seek re-election as a Conservative because he could not ask voters "to vote for policies which are directly opposite to those for which we all stood in 1970 and which I myself have consistently

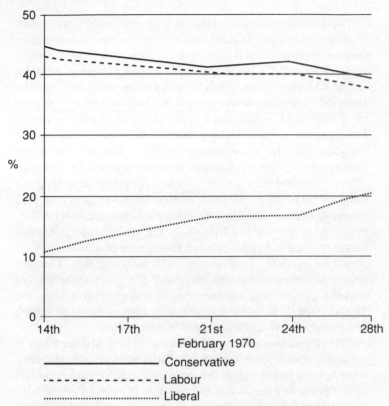

Fig. 6.1 Changes in party support during the February 1974 campaign
Source: Based on Gallup figures, *Daily Telegraph* and *Sunday Telegraph*.

condemned". The polls suggest that Labour was always running slightly behind the government, and that both lost support to the Liberals as the campaign went on (Figure 6.1), implying that the electorate was unconvinced by either of the major parties. Some polls gave the Liberals as much as 28% at one point, which was an exaggeration, but 25% and fifty seats were confidently expected. The two major parties did not seem to be worried, each assuming that the Liberals were taking more from their rivals.

The Liberals were well placed in England and Wales to profit from the electorate's distrust, and throughout the campaign they stressed themselves as the major alternative to the major parties. Because Jeremy Thorpe's majority in 1970 had been so small he decided to stay in his North Devon constituency and run the Liberals' campaign from there. This helped them to remain aloof from the London-based battle of the two major parties. A late injection of cash enabled them to field candidates in 517 constituencies, far more than in 1970. A sign that the major parties were taking the Liberals seriously was the invitation to Thorpe to join Heath and Wilson in talks aimed at settling the miners' strike. Unlike the other parties, the Liberals gave serious attention to the possibility of a hung Parliament, and what they might do if approached by one of the party leaders. All this meant that the Liberals achieved far more media coverage than they had in 1970. In a survey 55% believed that Thorpe's television appearances had increased his party's chances of winning a substantial number of seats and possibly holding the balance, and 35% found him the most impressive party leader, compared with Heath's 25% and Wilson's 18%.

The picture was different in Scotland. There had been less of a Liberal revival there during this Parliament, and the Liberals were fighting less than half the seats, so that the main beneficiary of the prevailing mood was the Scottish National Party (SNP). They had recovered rapidly from their poor showing in 1970 and had averaged nearly one-third of the vote in the four by-elections in Scotland since 1970. Their principal aim was independence for Scotland, with devolution merely a step towards it. This had been impractical up to now because Scotland could not afford to be independent, but the recognition that North Sea oil was a profitable proposition removed this obstacle, and the SNP was quick to claim what they termed "Scotland's oil".

The result

The opinion polls before polling day suggested that the Conservatives held a small lead over Labour, probably about

1%. On the day itself the turnout was high, particularly in the morning, and eventually reached 78.1%, the highest since 1951: this encouraged hopes that Labour voters had turned out, and this expectation was encouraged by exit polls showing a small swing to Labour. The Conservatives' own polls were optimistic, and the Liberals were looking for an increase on their latest poll showing of around 20%. Thus it would be true to say that all three parties were disappointed by the result, and in the case of Conservatives and Labour, unprepared. In votes, the Conservatives did have the largest share, but their 37.8% represented a loss of 1.27 million compared with 1970 and gave them only 297 seats, while Labour had secured 301 for their 37.1%, itself representing a loss of 530,000. Without the boundary changes which operated for the first time in this election, Labour would have won 40 seats from the Conservatives instead of the 24 they actually took. The Liberals had seen their vote almost treble, to over 6 million, had lost only two deposits (polled less than 12.5%) in England, where their share of the vote averaged 24% and had come first or second in 51 of the 76 seats along the south coast from Kent to Cornwall. Even so, they had fallen short of the level needed for a real breakthrough with 19.3%, and were as usual disadvantaged by the voting system, holding only 14 seats, which in fact involved losing both Ripon and Sutton and Cheam of their 5 by-election gains.

With three parties involved, the concept of "swing" becomes fairly misleading. The "average" was 0.9% to Labour, but the male vote showed a swing of 2.2% to the Conservatives, women 3.7% to Labour. The 35–44 age group showed a swing of 5.4% to Labour, the 45–54 5.2% to the Conservatives. Analysis by class, sex and age shows how substantially the Liberal vote had risen (see Figure 6.2).

The results in the regions were also very significant. The rise in Scottish nationalism was confirmed: the SNP won 21.9% of the vote in Scotland, nearly double their showing in 1970, and seven seats. In Wales Plaid Cymru's success was less remarkable, but they won two seats, even though their 10.7% share of the Welsh vote was slightly less than in 1970.

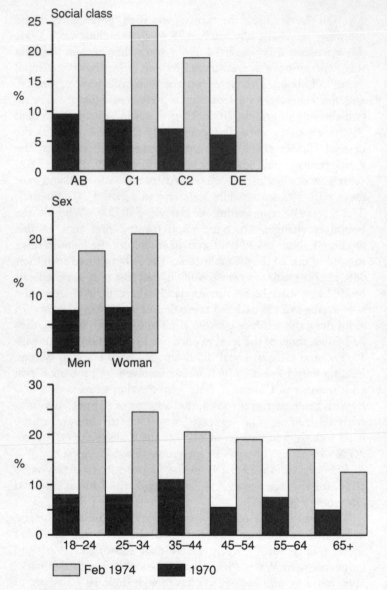

Fig. 6.2 Support for the Liberal Party 1970–February 1974

From the point of view of electoral arithmetic Northern Ireland is also very important. Since the partition of Ireland by the Government of Ireland Act in 1920 the twelve Northern Irish MPs had traditionally supported the Conservatives, something reflected in the full title of Conservative and Unionist Party. Even in 1970, two years after the start of the civil rights campaign eight Northern Ireland MPs took the Conservative whip, and there were seven at the dissolution. The 1970–1974 Parliament had seen immense changes in the political landscape of Northern Ireland. This is not the place to go into detail: from the point of view of the February 1974 General Election the most significant development was the series of agreements, sometimes known as the Sunningdale Agreement, between the British government, the Irish government and Northern Ireland politicians as to the system to replace the old Stormont. This would involve a "power-sharing" executive with both Catholic and Protestant ministers involved in governing Northern Ireland, under the leadership of Brian Faulkner, a constituent assembly elected by the Single Transferable Vote to devise a permanent political solution, and regular consultations between Great Britain, Northern Ireland and the Republic through a Council of Ireland.

The whole package met with a decisive rejection from Protestants in Northern Ireland. The most damaging response was the wave of strikes which included power workers at the Ballylumford power station, which could easily have halted the whole of Northern Ireland's industry, something fatal to any attempt to build a secure economic base for political initiatives. The verdict was the same in the General Election: candidates opposing power-sharing took 53% of the vote, and throughout Northern Ireland Protestant supporters of the Sunningdale Agreement were defeated by opponents. Of the twelve Northern Irish MPs elected in February 1974, eleven opposed the agreement, and the twelfth, Gerry Fitt, normally supported Labour in the House of Commons. Thus it is not surprising that Edward Heath's attempts to reach some sort of deal with the Ulster Unionist leader Harry West were decisively rebuffed.

Heath had also tried to reach an agreement with the Liberals. They were prepared for overtures to be made, and had said during the campaign that they were prepared "to work with any person of moderate and progressive views". Neither Jeremy Thorpe nor the grass-roots membership believed that Heath altogether fitted this description, though since there is no firm evidence on what the Liberals wanted as the price of their support, no verdict is possible on whether they deliberately pitched their demands too high. Certainly they wanted a Speaker's Conference on Electoral Reform, and it seems likely that they wanted more Cabinet posts in any coalition than Heath was prepared to give.

Even with the Liberals' 14 seats, assuming that all the Liberal MPs would have been prepared to go along with a leadership decision, Heath would have had only 311 seats, well short of an overall majority. On their own the Conservatives could have drawn up a Queen's Speech and challenged the opposition to defeat it, something for which there were several historical precedents, indeed it was the norm for much of the nineteenth century. The hard fact was that the Conservatives had lost far more support than any of the other parties, and had completely failed to gain the mandate for which Heath had appealed during the campaign. Once the results were complete Wilson had declared that he ought to be Prime Minister: after a weekend of discussions and abortive deals Heath reached the same conclusion, and Wilson was invited by the Queen to form a minority government, the first since 1929.

What happened?

It is perhaps a little arrogant for a writer on politics to claim that the answer to any question is easy, but in this case there is little doubt. One simple statistic tells the whole story: at the beginning of the campaign around 90% of voters questioned supported Conservative or Labour, whereas three weeks later less than 75% did. In England and Wales the Liberals picked up what the other parties lost, while in Scotland the SNP did likewise.

Though there were a few localised episodes, such as the swing of 16% to Labour in "Powell country", this was a campaign dominated by national issues, and crucially by a steady loss of confidence. It may be that the unexpected calling of a General Election fifteen months before it was needed caught a number of voters unprepared. On the other hand the high turnout suggests that many people wanted to emphasise the point of view that they did not have confidence in the two major parties. Both Conservative and Labour were seen as too similar: in outlook, policies and a tendency to go in for mud-slinging rather than genuine political debate. Such voters were not really concerned if the outcome was indecisive. Similar success for third parties and parties of protest was seen in other European countries at about this time, and it has been suggested that inflation was a common cause, though this is hardly likely to have been the case in Switzerland. Certainly many voters in the United Kingdom felt cut off from the political process: one opinion poll found that 88% of those questioned believed that things were being handled badly, but 60% felt frustrated that their opinions were not being taken into account.

The paradox is that the result inevitably meant that there would have to be another General Election very soon, almost certainly with the same leaders and attitudes. This may explain why the General Election of February 1974 left the voters slightly appalled at what they had managed to achieve.

7

The General Election of October 1974

Background

The only certain result of the February 1974 election had been that the minority Labour government could not hope to govern for very long, and therefore there would have to be another General Election soon. This raised a number of constitutional questions. If the government were defeated on a major issue, such as the Queen's Speech and Wilson resigned, would the Queen be justified in refusing to dissolve Parliament and in inviting Heath or another politician to try to form a government? There were precedents for a party other than the largest forming a government with the support of another party: the first Labour government in 1924 had been formed under those circumstances. In 1974, however, things were different, since the Liberals had only fourteen seats, and were not interested in a coalition with the Conservatives, certainly under Heath. Wilson himself has subsequently said that he would have gone to the country if defeated on the Queen's Speech, which was scheduled for 12 March, barely a fortnight after polling day, evidently assuming that the Queen would no longer exercise her constitutional right to refuse a dissolution. In the event the Conservatives let him off that particular hook by deciding not to oppose the government's programme, recognising that it was at best an interim measure. Wilson was much more concerned with the possibility that a fourth successive contest with Heath would simply be a recipe for boredom and apathy on the part of the electorate: on the other hand there was considerable moral pressure to go for an overall majority in order to carry out the programme the Labour Party believed necessary.

Apart from the role of the monarch, this period raised another constitutional issue: what was a government defeat? In fact Labour was defeated twenty-nine times in June and July, but did not resign as a result, and Wilson made it clear that he would only resign over an issue of confidence, and that it was his decision what that might be, something very far removed from textbook orthodoxy. In the event Parliament did not meet again after rising for the summer recess on 31 July: it was announced on 18 September that polling day would be 10 October. This was thus the shortest Parliament since 1681, and the first occasion since 1910 that there had been two General Elections in one calendar year.

In spite of the short interval between General Elections, there had been time for quite a lot to happen. Labour had made the greatest headway: in the short term they had settled the miners' strike, ended the three-day week and repealed the Industrial Relations Act, and in the longer term plans were announced for extending the public sector by nationalising aircraft building and ship building and repairing; granting a considerable measure of devolution to Scotland and Wales, in line with the 1973 Kilbrandon Report; and negotiating a "Social Contract" with the unions involving wage restraint by workers in return for price restraint and greater spending on welfare.

Some ministers had been warning that there could be no increase in living standards, but the government's economic strategy seems to have been directed as much against possible recession as against inflation: the Conservatives' Phase III was allowed to continue, pensions were increased, there were subsidies on food and to nationalised industries, and in his "mini-budget" just before the summer recess Denis Healey had cut the rate of Value Added Tax (VAT), introduced the previous year. The Conservatives did not oppose these proposals, but there were accusations outside Parliament that the government was manipulating the economy for short-term political advantage. Additionally Labour had taken advantage of being in government with a team of ministers with substantial experience of office (unlike 1964) to use the Civil Service to turn manifesto commitments into practical plans: Wilson recognised that in February the vote had been against Heath rather than for any concrete Labour programme. There were disagreements within Labour's National Executive Committee (NEC), and a number of allegations about personal and financial matters involving Wilson and some of his immediate staff and their families, but there was little obvious damage.

The Conservatives had lost support steadily since the February election. There was no immediate challenge to Heath as leader, but losses in the General Election had weakened the front-bench team as well as lowering morale. Surveys showed the extent to which they were still blamed for the confrontation leading to the February election, and it was clear that the electorate's faith in the Conservatives' ability to govern had declined seriously: in February they had been seen as more competent than Labour on over half the key issues, but by October they were behind on every issue.

The Liberals were disappointed by the February result, when they believed they were close to a breakthrough. Many were worried that the discussions with the Conservatives would suggest to those who had voted for them in February that they shared Conservative attitudes and policies, whereas many of the Liberal executive would have preferred an association with Labour. There was also disagreement about the possibility of a coalition if there were to be another hung Parliament, with the usual conflict of interest between independence and power. Jeremy Thorpe and David Steel were much more enthusiastic about a coalition than most of their Liberal partners. The Liberals had even lost one of their major issues. They had been advocating devolution for Scotland and Wales long before it became fashionable, but the government had now committed itself to legislate, and in Scotland the SNP were seen as the main party of devolution. They and Plaid Cymru were probably the most optimistic of the parties as the election approached: their major aim had been taken up by a party able to do something about it, they could claim that the problems were *England*'s rather than Scotland's, and their vote had shown that they had to be taken seriously by all the major parties.

The campaign

The October 1974 campaign was bound to be low key to the point of boredom: as Oscar Wilde's Lady Bracknell said of the end of the London season, people had already said everything they had to say, which in most cases was not much. The issues were the same as February, and it seemed to make little difference that it was now a Labour rather than a Conservative government that was asking for a renewed mandate: there was not much confidence that either party would be able to tackle the problems effectively. Labour laid some emphasis on the Social Contract in their manifesto, but otherwise there was agreement between them and the Conservatives that inflation was the main problem, and both parties had much more to say about Scotland than in February. For the Conservatives the problem was to find a new direction without admitting that they had been wrong in the past: their problems were not helped by the leaking of their manifesto on 10 September.

The Liberals did not even attempt to produce a new manifesto, merely adding a supplement to what they had used in February. At least they produced the most bizarre episode of the campaign. It was solemnly announced that "a major Labour figure" was joining the Liberals. When it turned out to be Lord St Davids, it was difficult to resist recalling the definition of journalists saying "Lord Jones dead" to people who did not know that he was alive. Certainly there was no benefit from this to the Liberals, who were annoyed by the tendency of the media to concentrate on their travel difficulties, such as Jeremy Thorpe's tour of coastal resorts by hovercraft.

Most of the "new" issues in the campaign had a slightly manufactured air. One such was the question of what was to happen if there was another hung Parliament after this election. This was not seen as particularly likely in view of the consistent lead of around 10% in opinion polls which Labour had held since March, but the Conservatives at least clung to the hope that there was some basis in fact for the *Daily Telegraph*'s claim that "the public seem to be tired of party warfare and to hanker after coalitions or centre groupings". Elsewhere in the press there was a noticeable shift away from the strong partisanship of the February election to a fairly strong endorsement of the middle ground if not of the Liberals. The Conservative manifesto referred to "a government of national unity", meaning not just a coalition, but a government containing major figures from outside the normal political scene: by implication the situation was as serious as in 1931 or 1940. The assumption was that this would be an alternative to Labour, but this raised the further question of Heath as leader of the Conservative Party, and more particularly whether a government of national unity would be easier to form if he stepped down. This was sometimes dubbed the "supreme sacrifice" argument, the patriotic figure giving up his position for the good of the country, but like so much else in this campaign it looked slightly phoney. If the Conservatives won, Heath's position would be safe and there would be no need for a coalition. If he did not, as Lord Boothby pointed out on polling day, the Conservatives are traditionally ruthless to losing leaders, particularly when, like Heath, they have lost three elections out of four. In any case, Labour were as opposed to coalitions as ever, and said so in their manifesto, and the Liberals were understandably unwilling to commit themselves in advance. The only practical outcome was that Heath attracted most of the coverage accorded to the Conservatives, though this may not have been a benefit since he had been trying to keep out of the limelight since February.

There were some difficulties for Labour over the Common Market, which with hindsight are significant. The government had embarked on the process of re-negotiating the terms agreed by the Heath government, and had promised to submit them to a referendum. Two of the party's most committed marketeers,

Shirley Williams and Roy Jenkins hinted that they might leave politics if the referendum produced a vote in favour of withdrawal. Writing about this later, Wilson believed that this drove a sizeable number of supporters of the Common Market away from Labour, but the result does not suggest that this made a significant difference, even assuming that many voters would regard their attitude towards the Common Market as decisive in choosing the next government.

There was also a considerable amount of dispute on the topic of inflation. Sir Keith Joseph, whose ideas were to shape the direction in which the Conservative Party went after this election, called for tighter control of the money supply as the only cure: this was largely rejected by most of his colleagues. Denis Healey claimed that the alarm about inflation was exaggerated, since it was standing at about 8.4%: the Conservatives responded by alleging a rate of over 30%: for the record, the figure was probably around 20%, though such figures are notoriously difficult to fix accurately. The electorate almost certainly took this as further evidence that the majority of politicians were not interested in solving the problems so much as in scoring points off their opponents, and that there was not much to choose between the parties in that respect. All this shows that it was very difficult for the parties to maintain any momentum, particularly over the last week of the campaign, and for the electorate to show very much interest. This, as much as the bad weather, explains why meetings were poorly attended. The media did not seem able to show much interest either: on television ITV, for example, gave less than half the coverage they had to the February election.

The result

There was much less coverage given to the opinion polls after their "failure" in February, which was a little unfair since they had largely been accurate in terms of votes, if not seats. As polling day approached, they were agreed that Labour should win comfortably, though there was a range from 4.5% to 14.5%

for the projected lead. On polling day exit polls (asking people
how they have voted as they leave the polling stations) suggested
that the Labour majority might be as high as 150 seats. On the
other hand the feeling among workers for both the major parties
was that the result would not be greatly different from February,
and this was confirmed by the private polls carried out for
Labour by Robert Worcester of MORI, who estimated a swing
to Labour of about 2.5%, which would give them a lead of about
50 over the Conservatives and an overall majority of between 5
and 10.

The turnout was expected to be low, and at 72.8% it was only
just above the post-war low of 1970. This represented a fall of
over 2 million compared with February (see Figure 7.1). Of
these the Conservatives lost 1.4 million, giving them easily their
lowest share of the vote since 1945 (35.8%); the Liberals lost
200,000 to fall back to 18.3%; Labour lost around 190,000,
giving them a share of the vote, at 39.2% that was their lowest
since 1935 and the lowest for any government with a majority
since 1922. Thus there had not been the Labour landslide
predicted by some of the polls, nor had the Liberals been able
to make a further advance from their February showing. In fact
they had increased their share of the vote in only 27 seats of the
145 where they had been second in February, so that their calls
for greater support had gone largely unheeded. Wilson later
claimed that the Liberal vote was seriously down and that this
harmed Labour: the results do not really support this point of
view, since all the "national" parties lost votes, and the Liberals'
loss seems to have benefited the other two equally.

In terms of seats, Labour had 319, a gain of 18, the
Conservatives had lost 20, at 277, and the Liberals' 13
represented a gain of 1 but a loss of 2. The swing to Labour
averaged 2.2%: if this had been uniform, they should have taken
25 marginals from the Conservatives, which would have given
them an overall majority of 17. Instead they took only 17, cutting
their effective majority to 3. One reason for this is that the
Conservatives had been expecting a summer election, and had
made a special effort in their highly marginal seats. By contrast

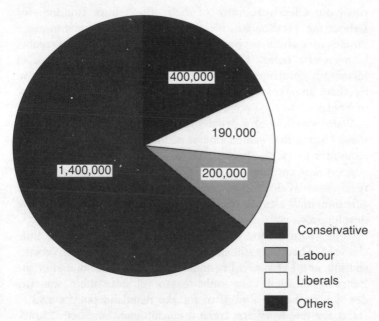

Fig. 7.1 Loss of support by all parties, February–October 1974

Labour's organisation had lost the enthusiasm of February. Membership was low, and local parties were increasingly unable to pay agents in the marginals where they were needed. Party workers were reluctant to turn out so there was less canvassing. This perhaps helps to explain why the polls once again overestimated the level of Labour support by anything up to 5%.

It was probably some consolation for Labour that their share of the vote in Scotland stayed steady, but the party which really succeeded was the SNP which carried on from where it had left off in February. It secured 30.4% of the vote in Scotland, an increase of 8.5%, almost entirely at the expense of the Conservatives, whose vote was down 8.2%, and won eleven seats in all. The problem for the Conservatives was to try to get the lost votes and seats back, which meant trying to build a more effective organisation in Scotland, since the rise of nationalism ruled out effective control of their efforts from London: for Labour the question was whether the SNP would start to make inroads on Labour support once they had taken all the available Conservative votes. This could threaten Labour's chances of forming a government, which depended on strong support in Scotland and Wales to offset their comparatively weak showing in England.

Wales was less of a problem for the major parties. Though Plaid Cymru had gained one seat, their share of the vote had risen only to 11.1%, barely back to their 1970 figure, and their support was confined to a small number of constituencies in rural west Wales. Even so, the government regarded the situation in Wales as justifying their plans for administrative devolution.

Voting patterns and the result in Northern Ireland were little changed. There was still strong opposition to any type of power-sharing, and Labour had re-imposed Direct Rule soon after the February election. The only feature of note there was the decision by Enoch Powell to forsake mainland politics and to stand for the Northern Ireland constituency of South Down. Otherwise he had very little impact, certainly not on the scale of the previous two elections. Complaints that he was merely using Northern Ireland as a base for a return to the national scene seriously misread the man, as his enthusiastic support for the Ulster cause confirmed.

What happened?

In both February and October only 75% of the electorate had voted Labour or Conservative. If this is further related to turnout, in February less than 59% of the electorate had supported either of the "parties of government", and in October it was less than 55%. People had lost confidence in either party to solve the United Kingdom's problems, quite simply, and it is not necessary to assume that some people decided not to vote Labour to prevent a landslide. This is part of a wider constitutional question which achieved great currency during the 1970s and is summed up in the title of a television series, "Is Britain becoming harder to govern?" The argument centred on the growing belief that all governments were imprisoned in a series of "dependency relationships": that there were so many interests on which government depended that they were almost totally unable to do anything on their own initiative. Some of these interests were international. The Conservatives had been unable to carry out their economic policy because of the oil-producing countries' decision to raise prices in 1973, and the pay pause had been disregarded by several multinational companies which had given pay rises well above the norm. Ever since the 1931 crisis the Labour Party had been suspicious of the City of London and the international financial system, especially the International

"Don't mention the election. He blames me because I stayed in to watch Porridge and Steptoe instead of going to vote."
© Express Newspapers plc

Monetary Fund, from which Labour had had to seek support between 1964 and 1970, when Harold Wilson blamed "the gnomes of Zurich" for many of the government's problems, as they also did after 1974. On the domestic scene, the Conservatives were seen as closely linked to big business interests, Labour as run to a great extent by the unions, or at least in their interest. Labour's manifesto commitment to work closely with the unions through the Social Contract reinforced this view, and as the Labour administration went on, events gave it even greater support. Wilson and the Labour leadership do not seem to have agreed: Wilson at least was convinced that they could continue to govern effectively for at least two or three years, even though a single-figure majority gave very little protection against probable by-election losses.

8
The General Election of 1979

Background

There is a widespread myth that Prime Ministers have a great advantage in being able to choose the date of the General Election. According to this, the economy can be manipulated to produce a favourable climate, and the pieces can be picked up afterwards. Leaving aside the question of whether government action can ever guarantee economic success, there is also the inconvenient fact that over a fifteen-year period the government of the day lost four of the six General Elections, those in 1964, 1970, February 1974 and 1979. Of these 1970 was probably the most surprising, but 1979 is the one where the timing of the election had the greatest effect on the outcome. Though success would not have been certain in September 1978, events over the next few months destroyed whatever chance Labour might have had.

Harold Wilson retired in the spring of 1976, characteristically quipping that he felt he ought to make way for an older man: he was replaced by Jim Callaghan, a politician of vast experience and the only post-war Prime Minister to have held all three of the top Cabinet posts, Chancellor of the Exchequer, Home Secretary and Foreign Secretary. Some people believed he was only a stop-gap, and there were strong hints of an election in September, but others, more prophetically, believed that he would want to enjoy the position for as long as possible, and he soon settled down in public esteem as probably the best "middle of the road" Prime Minister available. The economic situation might also have forced an election when a Treasury attempt to manage a devaluation got out of hand, the pound collapsed and the government had to go for support to the International Monetary Fund, which as usual imposed stringent conditions. The Chancellor, Denis Healey, threatened an election on the issue of "the IMF versus the people", but Callaghan made it clear that there was no chance of a repetition of 1951, and he had no intention of going to the country at that stage.

Another problem for the government in 1976 was that their fragile majority disappeared as a result of several by-election losses and the decision by Jim Sillars and John Robertson to form the Scottish Labour Party in order to press the government on devolution. In fact the government was not placed under too much pressure. They still had a comfortable lead over the Conservatives, who had not made a great deal of headway following the change of leader in February 1975 when Margaret Thatcher replaced Edward Heath. In addition Callaghan was able to carry out the same manoeuvre as Robert Walpole had done in the early eighteenth century, keeping the potential opposition divided by a series of promises which would fail if the government fell. Both the nationalist parties, with fourteen seats between them, would support the government until devolution could be achieved, and the Northern Ireland MPs, some of whom did not bother to attend the House, were kept happy by the promise of five additional MPs for Northern Ireland and a natural-gas pipeline. The Liberals went through a difficult period in 1976, when Jeremy Thorpe resigned as leader amid several scandals and their support in surveys and by-elections fell sharply from their 1974 position. In March 1977 the new leader David Steel agreed in principle to a pact between Labour and the Liberals which enabled the government to win fairly comfortably when the Conservatives moved a vote of no confidence. Thus by the summer of 1978 the government seemed to be well established, with an incomes policy that was generally accepted, and faced by a Conservative party whose policy documents had made little impact. The opinion polls confirmed both the strength of the government and difficulties for the Conservatives: some were suggesting that there would be greater support for the Conservatives under Heath rather than Thatcher.

There was some speculation about a General Election in 1978 as early as March, and the unions established "Trade Unions for a Labour Victory" in May. Some Conservatives were expecting a June election, but the strongest support outside the Cabinet was for October. If the government waited until 1979 there would be a plethora of elections, with local elections in parts of England, the devolution referendums in Scotland and Wales, and the first direct elections to the European Parliament. Callaghan's own account shows that he gave considerable thought to the timing of the election. On the credit side party morale was good, and an increased majority would end the niggling parliamentary defeats on minor issues; there were some in the Cabinet who favoured October, though only one who believed that a win was likely. The weight of argument was against, even setting aside Callaghan's natural caution. The Chief Whip, Michael Cocks, and the Whips themselves believed that the Conservative lead in the polls would make it difficult for Labour to win marginals in the Midlands or the north of England, and local results suggested that Labour might even lose some of the Midlands seats they had won in October 1974. An autumn election might also look like the government running away before things got worse. Callaghan seems to have made up his mind by mid-August, but he did nothing to damp down speculation until 7 September when in a broadcast he announced his belief that a general election at that stage would do the country no good. In his own mind he had settled on 5 April 1979, and his decision to delay the election was apparently vindicated by opinion polls showing Labour 5.5% ahead of the Conservatives as against a Conservative lead of over 6% a couple of months earlier, and well on course to win in April.

Callaghan's caution was to be severely punished. The government had effectively imposed a wage policy from 1975, and so far it had been accepted by the unions. The limit of a £6 rise for the year 1975–1976 had been seen as helping the low paid, and subsequent limits of 4.5% in 1976–1977 and 10% in 1977–1978 had been instrumental in bringing down inflation. The Chancellor's decision to recommend a 5% limit for the year 1978–1979 was economically justifiable but politically disastrous since it looked like a cut, and there was a strong mood at this time that people had a right to a steadily rising standard of living. It was decisively rejected both by the TUC and by the Labour Party Conference, and there was a feeling that there had been enough restraint since the crisis was well under control: one conference resolution rejected totally "any wage restraint by whatever method including cash limits, and specifically the government's 5%". The main practical response was the decision by unions in the public sector, such as the National Union of Public Employees (NUPE) to stage a series of strikes which lasted for six weeks from 3 January 1979, a period now usually known as the "Winter of Discontent". Some of the things which happened appalled even committed trade unionists, and politicians on both sides have referred particularly to the strike by grave-diggers in Liverpool which led to mourners being turned away from cemeteries, and the apparent refusal of NUPE's General Secretary to ask them to return to work.

The Conservatives made the expected political capital out of this, while for the general public the government's claim to be the only party which could guarantee the support and co-operation of the unions was shattered. It looked at times as though unions were able to take any action they liked, especially in the field of picketing without any legal restraint.

As in 1974 the industrial relations climate had a general effect on perceptions of the government, but what brought it down in 1979 was the issue of devolution, which had presented problems right through the Parliament. Initially the very different proposals for Scotland and Wales had been put into one Bill, but that had collapsed when the government was defeated on a guillotine motion. The measures were re-introduced in 1977 in two Bills, but by that time the government's majority was so shaky that the opponents of devolution were able to do a great deal of damage. The main time-bomb was planted by George Cunningham and Tam Dalyell: the Acts would only be put into operation if there was a vote in favour of devolution equivalent to 40% of those entitled to vote. The opponents of devolution were clearly assuming that though there was a lot of support, particularly in Scotland, it would fall short of the figure they imposed. The referendums took place on 1 March. In Wales there was a decisive rejection, fuelled by the large number of people who resented the impositions of a noisy minority, such as compulsory teaching of Welsh in all primary schools even in areas where Welsh was not spoken. The result in Scotland, however, was thoroughly unsatisfactory. Of those who voted 52% were in favour, but because 36% had failed to vote this represented only 33% of the electorate and the Act lapsed. Even the opponents of devolution were annoyed, arguing that too many people had believed that staying at home was the same as voting "No". If such people had turned out, they believed, devolution would have been defeated in Scotland as well: as it was, the pro-devolution lobby could claim "victory" in theory if not in practice.

This result destroyed Callaghan's hopes that he might delay a General Election until memories of the winter had worn off. The SNP announced that they would bring the government down unless there was a new vote in the House of Commons on devolution, and that they did not propose to discuss the matter further. They put down a motion of "no confidence", which Callaghan described as "turkeys voting for an early Christmas". The Conservatives endorsed this, and though the arithmetic remained uncertain until the end, the government was defeated on 28 March by one vote, 311 to 310, the first time since the war that a government had been brought down in the House of Commons. Callaghan decided on a General Election rather than advising the Queen to send for Mrs Thatcher. The parties agreed to allow essential legislation to be passed, including the budget, before the House rose on 7 April, and Polling Day was set for 3 May, the same day as local elections in parts of England.

The campaign

There were five weeks between the government defeat and polling day, a longer period for campaigning than earlier elections in the 1970s, but the Conservatives decided not to start until after Easter, thus cutting their campaign in half. Labour, on the other hand, were fairly happy with a long campaign, believing that most voters would make up their mind late, as had happened in 1970, and that in a long campaign Mrs Thatcher's lack of experience and her nerve would be tested.

Most of the campaigning took place on television, and was designed for it. This was partly the result of greatly increased security with the escalation of the "troubles" in Northern Ireland and the extension of the IRA campaign to the mainland. The House of Commons had received a violent reminder of this with the murder on 30 March of Airey Neave, the Conservative spokesman on Northern Ireland, and architect of Mrs Thatcher's leadership victory in 1975, blown up in his car as he left the underground car park at Westminster. There was also agreement between the parties that television was a much more important means of getting people noticed than meetings or rallies, and the Conservatives' Gordon Reece concentrated on making Mrs. Thatcher effective, though she caused something of a stir by refusing to appear in a televised debate with Callaghan and David Steel, apprehensive that the process of making the programme and its results would obscure the issues, as had sometimes happened in similar debates between presidential candidates in the United States. In spite of this suspicion Mrs Thatcher proved a very competent television performer, setting a trend which continued throughout her time as Prime Minister. The nature and timing of the daily press conferences were geared to television rather than newspapers, who were often reduced to reporting what politicians had said on television. This had the effect of reducing the impact of local issues and campaigning even more: what happened locally essentially echoed the national campaign.

Something very odd happened with the manifestos. Although Callaghan had succeeded in outflanking the left wing on

Labour's NEC and getting the sort of manifesto he wanted, it largely disappeared from view during the campaign, and all the debate centred on the Conservative manifesto, creating the strange situation of the government attacking the opposition's proposals. Thus Shirley Williams attacked plans for education and the Health Service, Joel Barnett listed the cuts in services that would result from Conservative tax plans, and the moderate leader of the Post Office Workers, Tom Jackson, described them as potentially the most extremist and reactionary government since the war. At a local level candidates often spent as much time talking about Mrs Thatcher as about Jim Callaghan, and there was a widespread feeling that Labour had not done enough in presenting a general vision and specific policies for the future, preferring to rely on an image of Callaghan as "Sunny Jim" which was sometimes hard to distinguish from blandness. By contrast the Conservatives, who used advertising agents Saatchi and Saatchi for the first time, targeted their campaign at specific weaknesses in the Labour record. One of their most effective posters showed a long queue of "unemployed" over the simple slogan "Labour isn't working."

The longer campaign meant more opinion polls. There had been a great deal of soul-searching and some changes among the polling firms after the apparent problems of 1970 and 1974, though it is difficult to know how much impact the polls actually had on the outcome. All agreed on giving the Conservatives a lead larger than any party had enjoyed at a comparable stage, and the bookmakers, sometimes an equally reliable guide, were offering odds of 4–1 on that the Conservatives would win. There was also broad agreement among the polls as the campaign went on that the Liberals were making a steady recovery: when the campaign opened they were below 5% but one poll was giving them 13% on polling day, and that turned out to be an underestimate. The decline of the nationalist parties was also clear, particularly in Scotland. There was rather more variation in the Conservative lead. One new organisation, which did not survive this election, was consistently giving the Conservatives a lead of 20%, but otherwise the range was generally between 5%

and 10%, with the exception of a nasty moment around the end of April when one poll on 28 April gave a Conservative lead of only 3% and three days later another showed a Labour lead of 0.7%. Robert Worcester of MORI later used this to support his view that politicians did not make enough use of polls in this campaign: both parties had abandoned daily private polls this time. According to Worcester, Labour's lead followed a speech pointing out what Conservative policies were likely to do to the Health Service, but no notice was taken of this in the Labour hierarchy, the issue was not pursued, and the Conservatives soon recovered their lead. Though there was a little unease at Conservative Central Office, there do not seem to have been the ructions that accompanied a similar episode in 1987.

The result

On polling day itself most polls gave the Conservatives a lead of 6%–8%, though the *Daily Telegraph* had them at 43% to Labour's 41%. The turnout was about 76%, an increase on October 1974, but that could have been the result of a newer register: the further away an election is from the compiling of the register in the autumn and its introduction in February, the more likely it is that significant numbers of voters will have died, or moved and so be ineligible to vote. Apart from the Liberals doing a little better than the polls had been suggesting, there were very few surprises, at least as far as votes were concerned. The Conservatives, with 339 seats had an overall majority of 43, but their share of the vote, 43.9% was the lowest for any post-war government apart from 1974, and only just over their post-war average, which suggests that they had regained the ground lost since 1974 but nothing more. Their strategy of trying to regain some of those who had voted Liberal in 1974 along with housewives from the C2 (skilled manual) group and first-time voters had been fairly successful. Mrs Thatcher's reference to the possibility of Britain being "swamped" by immigrants also had some effect on C2 voters, who feared job losses. This marked a departure from the tacit agreement during the 1970s that the parties would not exploit immigration as an election issue. On the other hand some analysts had been suggesting that the natural level of support for the Conservatives was 42%–43% and that this would condemn them to permanent second place in the electoral race. Labour won 268 seats, but had only 36.9%, their lowest since 1931: without a better than average showing in marginals, they would have lost even more seats than they did. On the other hand relations between the Parliamentary Party and the party organisation in Transport House were probably as bad as they had ever been, and many Labour politicians had given up hoping that Transport House might be effective in winning votes. All this made the "two-party" vote at 81%, the lowest so far apart from 1974.

The Liberals were once again disappointed. They had recovered considerably from their low point in 1976, but their 13.8% of the vote suggested that they had kept only about one-third of what they had gained between 1970 and 1974. Even so their share was the highest since 1929, with the exception of 1974. The voting system ensured that they had only eleven seats, which was a long way from their hopes of holding the balance. Like Labour they had not been able to put agents into all the key marginals where they were needed, and there is little doubt that the pact with Labour had some adverse effects at a local level.

The real losers were the nationalist parties. In Scotland support for the SNP had fluctuated according to the state of the devolution debate, and once the issue had been settled for the time being by the referendum result, there was little left. Even their exploitation of football turned sour. The SNP had made great capital out of the fact that Scotland was the only British team in the 1978 World Cup Finals in Argentina: after the Hamilton by-election in May 1978 where they came second to Labour, a telegram urged "next stop Argentina", to the great annoyance of other politicians. Humiliation for Scotland on and off the field may have helped to undermine the SNP still further. The fall in the vote, to 17.3% in Scotland was bad enough; worse still, they lost nine of their eleven seats. The Conservatives had suffered most from the rise of the SNP in the early 1970s, but they did not benefit to the same extent from their collapse: their share of the vote in Scotland of 31.4% showed a greater rise than Labour, but was still below February 1974 and well down on 1970. In addition they lost their last seat in Glasgow. In Wales there was a fall in the Plaid Cymru vote, though not as drastic as the equivalent in Scotland: their 8.1% led to the loss of one of their three seats. The Conservatives did benefit here, with their highest number of Welsh seats since 1874, mainly because they were the only party to oppose devolution.

The mid-1970s had seen something of a revival for the National Front, mainly on the immigration issue. Their showing in by-elections had led them to mount a sustained campaign in this election, with 303 candidates. Outside the cities of London and Leicester they polled extremely badly, gaining only two or three hundred in most places. In Dover a "Silly Party" candidate who stood to ridicule the National Front scored twice as many votes. It is possible that some voters who were afraid that high immigration would further increase unemployment were re-assured that a Conservative government would impose limits. On the other hand much of the National Front vote before 1979 had been a one-off protest.

The average swing to Conservatives over the country was 5.1%, a post-war record, but this concealed wide variations. There was a small swing to Labour in Scotland, and lower than average swings in cities with a high immigrant population perhaps reflecting apprehension over Conservative intentions. The highest swings were in the south, averaging over 7%, with around 11% in south and east London.

What happened?

In their first Party Election Broadcast the Conservatives used the phrase "We all know in our hearts it is time for a change"; after the election Labour analysts said that British politics undergoes a sea-change every thirty years or so. 1979 saw just such a change. Among the causes the main specific factor was the Winter of Discontent and its aftermath: the events of some of the strikes had alienated many trade unionists, and increased the feeling that unions ought not to be so totally free from legal restraints as they appeared to be. The Conservatives offered the only prospect of such restraints being applied, and as a result significant numbers of workers swung from Labour to Conservative, 11% in the case of C2 (skilled manual workers and their wives) giving the Conservatives 40% as against Labour's 42%, and 9% among DE voters, meaning that at 49% Labour had less than half of any of the working class vote for the first time since the war (see Fig. 10.2). Confirmation that workers as much as wives were affected comes from the finding that the swing to Conservative was 4% among women and 7% among men.

In general terms there was clear support for the Conservative style. In all sorts of ways the pragmatism of both parties in the 1970s had produced nothing but trouble, particularly in the economy. To take just one example, the increase in wages in real terms, at 1.5% was less than half the average for the rest of the Common Market. This time the Conservatives had presented their general philosophy as much as a shopping list of proposals, and had stressed that this election represented the last chance to restore the balance between the state and the individual and to bring back the approach to political activity which would soon become known as Thatcherite. In fact, though, the Conservatives did not concentrate their campaign on Mrs Thatcher in the way that Labour focused on Callaghan. Surveys suggested that he was much the more popular as a leader, but as had been clear in 1945, for example, our electoral system does not always produce a "presidential" outcome.

There was another general explanation for the 1979 result, and it helps to justify the verdict that it was a watershed election. At some time during the 1970s, nobody knows exactly when, the whole basis of voting behaviour had become more volatile. This topic is dealt with in Chapter 17, but 1979 was the first election in which it became probable that all the old assumptions about the factors affecting the way people vote had ceased to operate in the ways to which psephologists had become accustomed over the post-war years. One striking example of this came with

the differing fortunes of two Labour ministers. Plymouth
Devonport, the seat of David Owen, Labour's Foreign Secretary
was very marginal, and on the swing recorded should have been
lost, whereas Shirley Williams was believed to be fairly safe in
Hertfordshire. Dr Owen spent the whole of the campaign
nursing his seat and won: Mrs Williams took a major role in the
London end of Labour's campaign and lost, which suggested
that constituents expected MPs to put their constituencies first.
Quite simply, since none of the parties could now rely on their
traditional class bases of support, they were going to have to
work for votes from now on.

9

The General Election of 1983

Background

According to one account, the prevailing view in the Labour Party after the 1979 election was that Mrs Thatcher would prove so reactionary and incompetent in government that Labour would easily return to power next time, following the pattern of the 1970s of one weak government being replaced by another. For nearly three years it looked as though this opinion was right. From the middle to the end of 1981 the Conservatives were consistently third in the opinion polls, and Mrs Thatcher's rating of 24% was the lowest for any Prime Minister or party leader since the war.

In part this was the result of the Conservatives' own problems. The 1970s had seen a serious and irreversible weakening in confidence on the part of voters: they no longer identified strongly with any party as had been the case in the 1950s and 1960s and no longer trusted governments to fulfil their promises. This was particularly true in the economy, where nothing seemed to have improved in comparison with Labour. Unemployment was still rising, reaching 3 million early in 1982, tight control of the money supply was causing immense damage to British industry and inflation was back at 20%, caused partly by two government decisions: the recommendations for wage rises by the Clegg Commission had been honoured, and VAT had been raised from 8% to 15% in the first budget after the election.

Another problem was Margaret Thatcher's style. Nobody in politics really knew what to expect when she was elected leader in 1975: the only Cabinet post she had held was Education Secretary under Heath, when she had been seen as one of the more high-spending ministers, and the main reason for her election had been that she was everything Edward Heath was not. She clearly knew what she did not like, principally union power and high public spending, and she was determined to get her own way, either in Cabinet or through Cabinet committees. One Cabinet minister of that period has said that she went through meetings in a permanent state of fury: whereas Heath had sulked when he could not get his own way, Mrs Thatcher raged, lashing into everybody who did not seem to share her view that British politics needed a radical transformation, not just a series of gentle adjustments. This had an effect on the Cabinet, where there was an atmosphere of barely suppressed disagreement and hostility, not helped by the unwise practice of one or two ministers trying to make jokes at Mrs Thatcher's expense. Several ministers used to dread attending Cabinet meetings, and none of them had any experience of conducting a political argument with a woman.

The nature of the Cabinet did not help. The group chosen in 1979 was broadly based, with a high proportion of people initially chosen by Heath, and expecting office as a reward for bearing the heat and burden of opposition whether they were capable of it or not. This built opposition into the Cabinet, and contributed to the verdict of one minister that it was one of the unhappiest and most divided of modern times. One consequence of this was that information tended to emerge in a series of leaks, and it was sometimes difficult to know whether a leak was official or unofficial. It was not until November 1981 that Mrs. Thatcher managed to prune what she regarded as the "dead wood" of such "one-nation Tories" as Sir Ian Gilmour, and to bring into the Cabinet people who shared her views, of whom the most notable were Norman Tebbit and Nigel Lawson.

At first the Labour Party was the principal beneficiary of these difficulties for the government, as was to be expected: by the last quarter of 1980 they were standing at about 50% in most opinion polls. But since the General Election defeat Labour had been engaging in the usual series of recriminations. Philip Snowden had described this in the 1930s as "one of those exhibitions of disloyalty and the lack of team spirit which have so often exposed the Labour Party to the jeers of its opponents and caused dismay among its supporters in the country". Harold Wilson had later compared the Labour Party to passengers in a stage-coach: too excited or sick while the coach is in motion to worry about what is happening, but once it stops all getting out to argue about where they are going. At the Labour Party Conference in 1980 there were three main complaints: that the election of the leader by MPs alone did not reflect the nature of the party as a whole; that the automatic re-selection of sitting Members might saddle a constituency with someone whose ideas were now totally at odds with the local membership or the national party; and that the writing of the manifesto by the leader and whoever he chose could mean that Labour would go into an election with a programme which left out or distorted a great deal of party policy. The conference refused to agree that the manifesto should be written by the NEC, but accepted the other two complaints. In future all sitting Labour Members would have to go through a re-selection process during the life of a Parliament, and the leader would be elected by an electoral college which would be more representative of the party, at least in theory. A special conference was held at Wembley in January 1981 to hammer out the details. Although most interests in the Labour Party were agreed that MPs should have at least half the votes in the electoral college, since a leader does most of his work in the House of Commons, a series of accidents and muddles produced an electoral college with 40% for the unions and 30% each for MPs and constituency parties. Michael Foot was endorsed as leader, having already been chosen by MPs to replace Callaghan, but major splits were revealed when Tony Benn decided to challenge Denis Healey as deputy leader, suggesting that the new procedures were unlikely to be less divisive than the old ones. The views of the general public

were expressed in opinion polls immediately afterwards, which
showed a fall in Labour's support of nearly 12%.

These problems for the Labour Party not only weakened its
position, they provided the impetus for the formation of a new
party. As long ago as 1979 Roy Jenkins had raised the idea of a
new centre party when he delivered the BBC's Dimbleby
Lecture: his view was that there was ample room for a party of
the radical centre which would command the support of many
of the electorate who were disillusioned by two "parties of
government" which had moved to their extremes. Not much had
happened immediately, but the events of 1981 made the idea
very attractive to the right wing of the Labour Party, particularly
those who supported the Common Market. They were afraid
that the introduction of mandatory re-selection would now make
it impossible for pro-marketeers to fight off attempts to unseat
them by their constituency parties, especially if they had been
taken over by a small group of dedicated left-wing anti-
marketeers, the phenomenon sometimes known as "entryism".

The stages by which the Council for Social Democracy and
the Social Democratic Party (SDP) came into being have been
well covered elsewhere: from the point of view of the next
General Election the important thing is that the new party was
ideally placed to capitalise on the situation prevailing when it was
launched in the early part of 1981. The Conservatives had still
failed to solve most of the more obvious problems; Labour was
mainly occupied in tearing itself to pieces; the Liberals were still
recovering from the disappointment of 1979, which had cost
them three major figures. The new party had attractive personalities in David Owen and Shirley Williams, and they had novelty
value, a great asset when so many of the electorate had lost
confidence in the established parties. Most important they had
something which third parties had lacked since the war,
experience of government: David Owen had been Foreign
Secretary, Roy Jenkins had been both Home Secretary and
Chancellor of the Exchequer before 1970, and both Shirley
Williams and Bill Rodgers had held office between 1974 and
1979. Their hopes of attracting a substantial number of MPs

from both parties were slightly disappointed when they attracted only one Conservative, but by the beginning of 1982 they had twenty-nine MPs, mainly Labour defectors who had had problems with their constituency parties and Shirley Williams had won the hitherto safe Conservative seat of Crosby. An agreement had been reached with the Liberals not to stand against each other in by-elections, though David Steel's suggestion that the logical place for Labour dissidents was the Liberal Party had not been followed up. Even so, the association with the Liberals gave the SDP a national organisation to supplement what was essentially a London-based party.

Then on 2 April the whole political scene was thrown into turmoil by the Argentine invasion of South Georgia and the Falkland Islands. This began badly for the government: the Foreign Secretary, Lord Carrington, resigned along with his two junior ministers, Humphrey Atkins and Richard Luce, and there were suggestions that things would have been even worse if the government's cuts in the navy had taken effect. Thereafter all the benefit went to the Conservatives. There was admittedly very little that Labour could offer as an alternative except insist that more use ought to be made of the United Nations, but this docs not explain what soon became known as the "Falklands Factor". A great deal has been written about this without making it very much clearer: it is one of those curious things in politics, in that we know what it did, we just do not know how it did it. It was certainly more complicated than the tabloid newspapers would suggest, with their insistence on bashing foreigners, though there was an element of that. In part people had become used to governments failing in international affairs, something perhaps going as far back as Suez in 1956, and reinforced by many of the problems of the 1970s. In addition, it changed the way in which the Tories in general and Mrs Thatcher in particular were viewed. Up to now their attitude had looked bloody-minded, with its insistence on not changing, particularly in the face of of rising unemployment and high inflation; as Mrs Thatcher had put it at the Party Conference, "You turn if you want to: the lady's not for turning." Now this refusal to budge looked steadfast and reliable, and perfectly caught the mood of the times, so that disagreement came to look almost unpatriotic. For Mrs Thatcher herself it enhanced her confidence and stature to the extent that she was transformed from an electoral liability into a major asset.

Even without the Falklands Factor the other parties were running into trouble by the latter part of 1982, though it is futile to speculate whether this would have enabled the Conservatives to win anyway. Labour had never really recovered from their internal problems: polls showed the party's image as divided, lacking credibility and weakly led, as in 1959, even among people sympathetic to them. Michael Foot's personal rating was the lowest for any party leader, partly because Labour was committed to a non-nuclear defence policy, which Foot had always supported, and partly because of his poor performances in Parliament and on television. The fairly regular demolition of Foot by Thatcher during Prime Minister's questions had become known as "hand-bagging". The decline in support for Labour was confirmed by a series of dismal by-election results, culminating in a drop of nearly 16% in Labour's vote in Crosby.

Though the SDP had won several seats, they too had difficulties involving their leadership. As the senior figure, Roy Jenkins was the natural choice to lead the party, but his four years as President of the European Commission had blunted his parliamentary skills, and he was badly affected by barracking from some left-wing Labour MPs who were not only opposed to the Common Market as such, they resented what they saw as Jenkins going off to a better-paid job when things were getting difficult for the Labour government.

In January 1983 the SDP staged a re-launch to try to regain the momentum they had lost after the Falklands conflict, and they got a further boost when they won the safe Labour seat of Bermondsey. This was another illustration of Labour's problems: the constituency party had selected the controversial Peter Tatchell as candidate: he was not only a left-winger, he was strongly committed to gay rights. Though Michael Foot had said that Tatchell would be a candidate "over his dead body", the fact that none of the party's rules had been broken meant that he was powerless to intervene.

From May 1982 the Conservatives were at least 10% ahead in the polls, having leapt to 50% immediately after the end of the Falklands War. They began mapping out their electoral strategy in January 1983. Boundary changes were due which Labour unsuccessfully challenged in the courts, but any chance that this might lead Foot to step down in favour of the more formidable Healey was quashed by the Labour victory in Darlington on 24 March, the Liberal/SDP Alliance coming a poor third. Inflation was falling and the rate of rise in unemployment was slackening, so Mrs Thatcher decided to call a General Election for 9 June even though the government had been in office for barely four years and though no twentieth- century government had won a June election. This is the sort of challenge she seems to relish. She dealt characteristically with Labour accusations of "cutting and running": "if you go between four and five years you are cutting and running. If you don't decide, you are dithering. If you continue to go the whole year you are clinging to office."

The campaign

There was almost total agreement from the start as to what would happen: the polls had the Conservatives between twelve and eighteen points ahead of Labour, with the SDP/Liberal Alliance at about 18%–20%. The bookmakers agreed, having the government 5–1 on, and Labour 7–2 against. There was little change during the campaign, though Labour picked up slightly in the first week, and lost ground to the Alliance in the second and third weeks; the Conservatives fell back slightly during the last week.

The Conservatives handled their campaign as though they were sure to win. In 1979 they had said that their manifesto was a programme for two Parliaments, so they concentrated on maintaining existing plans. Francis Pym worried that too big a majority would be a liability: his remarks were dismissed by the Prime Minister as "a typical Chief Whip's concern" before the election, and Pym himself was dismissed shortly afterwards. Mrs Thatcher featured strongly, taking all the London press conferences, and the party organisation made considerable use of new technology such as direct mail and computers.

Although the Conservatives made some ritual attacks on Labour's plans, they probably need not have bothered since Labour did a fairly good job of destroying their own prospects. 46% of respondents in a survey felt that the campaign had harmed Labour's chances, and it has more recently been described as "the most incompetent of any major political party in a Western democracy in the post-war world". Lack of funds had forced Labour to move their headquarters away from Transport House to Walworth Road though they still held their press conferences in Smith Square, and neither the National Agent nor the Director of Publicity had fought an election before. The unsuccessful challenge to the boundary changes had left eighty selections still to complete, and some candidates had to go through the process again. The manifesto was summed up by Peter Shore, a former Labour minister as "the longest suicide note in history", mainly because there was nothing in it to suggest any new ideas, and the electorate was bound to reject it. Michael Foot even attacked Lord Hailsham over his conduct during the Munich crisis in 1938. This reinforced the realisation very early that Michael Foot was an electoral liability: in polls his ratings for leadership, personality and effectiveness in a crisis were in single figures. Unfortunately nothing could be done about it. Jim Mortimer's well-meant attempt to boost Foot's credibility by asserting that "the unanimous view of the campaign committee is that Michael Foot is the leader of the Labour Party" did not help; neither did Callaghan's public repudiation of the party's defence policy on 25 May, and remarks by Denis Healey and Neil Kinnock about Mrs Thatcher's attitude to the Falklands War.

There were also problems for the Alliance. Even before the campaign there had been difficulties in allocating seats to the respective parties, with some Liberals being reluctant to work for an SDP candidate who, as the Labour MP, they had previously been trying to unseat. There had been criticism from some senior Liberals of the speed with which the manifesto had been produced, and the usual lack of funds had virtually prevented national advertising. As in the Labour Party, leadership was a weakness. The Alliance had put forward Roy Jenkins as "Prime Minister designate", but he did not show up well in comparison with either David Steel or David Owen, and provoked negative reactions even from SDP candidates. A crisis meeting was held at Steel's home in Ettrick Bridge, and though it failed to persuade Jenkins to step down entirely, he did agree to take a relatively minor role from then on.

The result

The exit polls conducted by both ITV and the BBC were amazingly accurate in seats as well as votes, and those psephologists who wanted an early night were able to get to bed well before midnight with the result certain. The turnout was low again, at 72.7%. More seriously, as most commentators pointed out, the result was the most distorted since 1918 in terms of the ratio of seats to votes. The Conservatives had won by a landslide in seats, their 397 being their largest number since the war and giving them an overall majority of 144. Yet they had only 42.4% of the vote, almost the lowest of any majority government ever and 700,000 less than in 1979. They did relatively better in the south and in rural areas, picking up votes from those who had not voted in 1979 and, more surprisingly, among first-time voters, traditionally likely to favour Labour. They even had 30% of the unemployed, and their share of C2 voters remained steady, though they did badly among non-whites and young unemployed, probably an overlapping group of whom many did not bother to vote.

Labour had done as badly as the polls and the campaign had indicated, and the voting system did at least reflect this. Labour lost 3 million votes in comparison with 1979, a third of their vote at that time. Of this 22% had gone to the Alliance, 7% to the Conservatives and a further 7% had abstained. Their share of the vote, at 27.6% was the lowest since 1918 and their share per candidate the lowest ever. Their net loss was 6.5% in Scotland

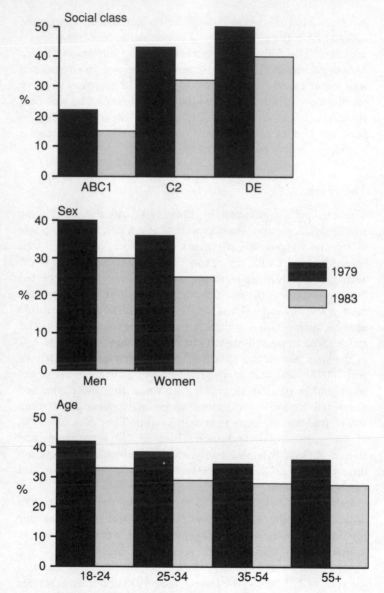

Fig. 9.1 Decline in Labour Party support, 1979–1983

and 6.8% in the north-west, but elsewhere their loss ranged from 9% to 12%, and averaged 9.3%. All the traditional measures, by class, age and sex showed a fall for Labour of between 6% and 11% (see Figure 9.1). Their number of seats, 209, was 49 less than in any post-war election, and they lost 119 deposits compared with a previous worst of 35. As an effective political force Labour had disappeared from the south of

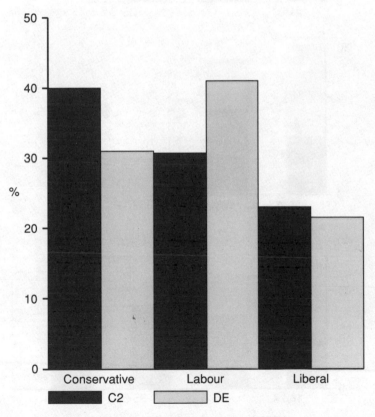

Fig. 9.2 Working-class votes, 1983

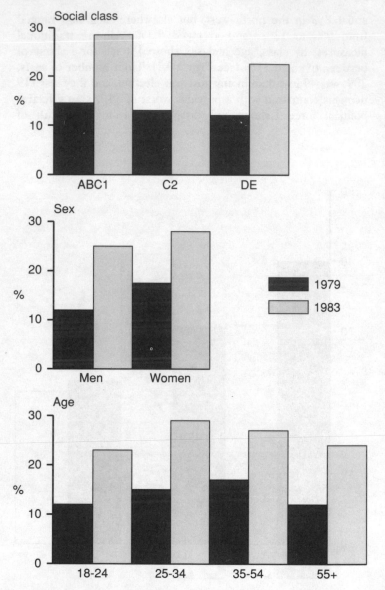

Fig. 9.3 Rise in Liberal/SDP Alliance support, 1979–1983

England: they were also apparently in the process of disappearing from the working class as well, since they polled only 32% of C2 voters and 41% of DE (see Figure 9.2). To add to their problems, the recent re-distribution of seats, which increased the size of the Commons from 635 to 650, had decreased greatly the number of marginal seats which Labour might win.

Third parties usually have good reason to be disappointed at the result of General Elections: in 1983 the Alliance were justified in being furious. They had won 25.4% of the vote, far more than in any post-war election, had come first or second in over half the contests, and their share of the vote had gone up between 10% and 14% according to class and age indicators, 10%–13% by region in England and Wales, 15.5% in Scotland where they profited by a further decline in the SNP (see Figure 9.3). Yet they had only 23 seats, and of the 29 with which the SDP had gone into the election they had retained only 6. It can have been little consolation that they had reduced the two-party vote to its lowest level ever. Both the nationalist parties had fallen back still further in votes by comparison with 1979, though neither had lost seats: the SNP had 11.8% of the vote in Scotland, Plaid Cymru 7.8% of the Welsh vote. The only

THE SUNDAY TIMES

An injustice that must not endure

notable feature in Northern Ireland was that the turnout was high, at 76%: otherwise the province continued to reflect its own concerns and to remain aloof from what was happening in the rest of the United Kingdom.

What happened?

Ivor Crewe's judgement on this election has passed into political folklore: "the electorate did not embrace the Conservatives; it rebuffed Labour and flirted with the Alliance". In spite of their apparent landslide, the Conservative share of the vote *fell* by comparison with 1979, in spite of their strategy of trying to keep the loyalty of those who had voted for them in 1979. Labour had clearly lost the support of the electorate on a massive scale. This was partly caused by long-term changes in voting behaviour, but there were factors peculiar to this election, particularly the leadership at the time, the apparent inability to control the left wing and policies on such issues as defence. Even the *Daily Mirror*, frequently the only newspaper to support Labour, was very doubtful, the *New Statesman*, Labour's main weekly was suggesting tactical voting (recognising that Labour could not win, and so voting for the party most likely to stop the Conservatives) and *Tribune*, traditionally the voice of Labour's "soft left", was warning during the campaign that the Labour Party had only a week to save itself from disaster. The *Daily Star* claimed that "[We] might have supported Labour IF it was united, IF the wild men had been thrown out and IF its nuclear policies had been more moderate", though in view of the generally anti-Labour nature of the British tabloid press such claims should be taken with a pinch of salt.

It is clear that about 80% of voters made up their minds early in the campaign, so that the Alliance difficulties in projecting their policies were probably of little importance. Significantly 15% of Alliance voters apparently made up their minds in the last couple of days of the campaign, as against 4% of Conservatives and 6% of Labour voters. The swing of 7% from Labour to Alliance probably represents a Labour loss rather than an Alliance gain. The Alliance suffered from something that might seem to be one of its greatest strengths, that its support was spread evenly over classes and regions rather than concentrated in one class or area. The other two parties can afford to come third in some seats as long as there are plenty where they will come first; but without a proportional voting system there is nothing to be gained from coming second.

10

The General Election of 1987

Background

The four years between the General Elections in 1983 and 1987 are a good illustration of the volatile and unpredictable nature of British politics since 1970. The opinion polls were particularly variable: in the autumn of 1983 the Conservatives had risen to 45%, the Alliance had fallen to 19% and Labour were in third place, whereas at the equivalent period in 1985 Labour were in the lead and the Alliance were at their highest level and the Conservatives down to 24%. Labour in fact were ahead for most of this Parliament, though they were always below 40%, a crucial barrier to possible electoral success.

The government's fortunes were especially changeable. They had remained largely accident-free in the run up to the 1983 election, but they certainly made up for it afterwards. William Whitelaw went as Leader of the House of Lords; in the resultant by-election at Penrith the government lost nearly 13% of their vote of only a month before. A few weeks later Cecil Parkinson, Secretary of State for Trade and Industry and one of the main architects of the 1983 success, resigned following a scandal about an extra-marital affair. A BBC "Panorama" programme alleged that there was a great deal of extreme right-wing support in the Conservative Party, both among some MPs and especially at grass-roots level, and though some of the people implicated by the programme were vindicated when they brought libel suits against the programme, they could not entirely dispel the suspicion about some parts of the party. The close relationship between Mrs Thatcher and President Reagan was called into question when the USA intervened to prevent a *coup d'état* in Grenada without apparently consulting the United Kingdom. Lord Whitelaw, one of the major "soothing" influences in the Conservative Party and apparently one of the few people to whom Mrs Thatcher listened, was given the job of steering the government around further "banana skins", but he could not prevent the House of Lords taking on the role of "alternative opposition" and inflicting a number of defeats on the government on such issues as rate-capping and the "Paving Bill" cancelling elections for the Greater London and Metropolitan Councils in preparation for their abolition. The government did hope that the end of the miners' strike in March 1985 would provide a "Falklands Factor" but the Brecon and Radnor by-election shattered such expectations, being their worst defeat since Orpington in 1962. It was particularly worrying that there was a mood of considerable pessimism in the constituencies.

At the beginning of 1986 came the Westland affair. Michael Heseltine, the Defence Secretary, walked out of the Cabinet on the grounds that the failure to take his views into account over the sale of the helicopter company was symptomatic of Mrs Thatcher's attitude to Cabinet government in general. Soon afterwards Leon Brittan, the Trade and Industry Secretary, felt compelled to resign when it was revealed that some of his civil servants had been used to undermine Heseltine's position on the consortium to take over Westland. For a time it looked as though the Prime Minister might become involved, since Brittan claimed to have had approval from Downing Street for the leaking of a crucial letter, and she herself said on the day of the crucial Commons debate "by six o'clock today I may no longer be Prime Minister". Not for the first time Neil Kinnock put up a weak performance and allowed the government to survive. It was still under pressure, however. On 14 April 72 Tory MPs rebelled to defeat the Sunday Trading Bill amid allegations that a deal had been made with Ulster MPs who were totally opposed to the Anglo-Irish Agreement made the previous November. At the same time the "special relationship" with the USA again caused controversy when British bases were used for a bombing raid on Libya. In May the government lost a by-election at Ryedale, and only narrowly held on in West Derby, confirming the view that in by-elections nowadays there are no safe seats for any party.

Meanwhile the Labour Party was rebuilding after the 1983 disaster. Michael Foot resigned almost immediately, and the party decided to skip a generation in electing the "dream ticket" of Neil Kinnock as leader with Roy Hattersley as his deputy. Kinnock began with a number of advantages. He was not associated with previous Labour failures in government; he looked good on television; and he recognised the need for Labour to adopt a new approach instead of trying to insist that the old one ought to work next time. As he put it, Labour had to appeal to the home-owner as well as the homeless, the stable family as well as the single parent, the confidently employed as well as the unemployed. Helped by a majority of eighteen to ten on Labour's NEC he was able to preside over a series of new policy initiatives designed to ensure that the party would go into the next election with a range of policies that had been considered, discussed, publicised and agreed well before the start of the campaign. Thus in August 1985 "A new partnership, a new Britain" was launched with the active co-operation of the TUC, which offered a detailed programme for the economy and job creation; the Freedom and Fairness campaign in the following April focussed on law and order, education and the Health Service, with the telling slogan "Be patient. There'll be a better health service along shortly"; and in September 1986 there were further discussions with union leaders offering the hope of a new Social Contract.

There were some problems. The government's enormous majority made opposition in the House of Commons a disheartening business, leading some of the Labour left to decide that it was pointless, and that the only way to challenge the government was outside Parliament. The miners' strike and

the activities of left-wing councils especially in London and
Liverpool were aspects of this approach, and Labour found it
difficult to cope with them. Thus the miners' strike halted
Labour's advance in the polls, and though Kinnock gained
considerable personal prestige from his attacks on the Militant
Tendency in general and Liverpool's Militant councillors in
particular, they left an uncomfortable feeling that he looked best
when he was attacking his own side. In general, though, Labour
were in better heart than at any time since 1979, and Neil
Kinnock could justifiably claim that Labour was much better
organised than in 1983 and much more effective at delivering its
policies. This was confirmed when they kept Fulham in a by-
election, the sort of seat that they might earlier have lost to the
Alliance.

The Alliance had also faced some difficulties in comparison
with the heady days of 1981–1983. As expected, Roy Jenkins was
replaced as leader of the SDP by David Owen – showing that
their democratic processes for choosing a leader could still bring
about a coronation – and the Liberal leader David Steel decided
to take a sabbatical after the pressure of the 1983 campaign.
They continued to do well in votes: at one point in the polls the
Alliance had 40% to 30% for each of the other two parties. In
by-elections the average for the Alliance vote rose by 25% while
Labour's fell by 16% and the Conservatives' by 49% compared
with 1983, but as usual for third parties it was less easy to convert
votes to seats. There were also problems with policy, and the
SDP was not the first party to discover that people who are
prepared to support a party on image or protest are less
enthusiastic once there are some clear policies to disagree with.
In April 1986 there were signs of a rift over education but the
most serious issue was defence. David Owen and the SDP
favoured retaining Britain's nuclear weapons. David Steel saw
this as a necessary part of retaining the Alliance, but at the
Liberal Party's Eastbourne Conference the unilateralist wing,
always a strong tradition in the party, succeeded in getting a
resolution passed in favour of a non-nuclear policy. Steel was not
pleased, Alliance support fell to its lowest level in the polls, and

in the view of one prominent Liberal the defence decision could have cost them the next election.

In retrospect the 1986 Conservative Party Conference marked the start of the campaign as far as the government was concerned. Conservatives were told to look for a third term in office, and more significantly, several new initiatives were begun, suggesting that they were aware of the danger of appearing to run out of ideas, and anxious to maintain their image of radicalism. Kenneth Baker secured the biggest cheer of the conference when he announced the creation of City Technical Colleges which would be independent of local authority control. After the summer recess public spending was allowed to overshoot the government's targets by £5 billion and in the 1987 budget the standard rate of income tax was cut by 2p in the pound. A scheme to dump nuclear waste underground in any of four possible sites, all of them in Conservative constituencies, was abandoned. As well as the benefits for the government which had come from effective political management and the economic upturn, Mrs Thatcher's personal standing had been greatly enhanced by her visit to the Soviet Union. Her image as a major world leader in the same league as the leaders of the super-powers was a significant advantage for the Conservatives during the campaign. By the beginning of May many Tories had already set off to begin their personal campaigns, and there was strong pressure from the media and from politicians for Mrs Thatcher to end the uncertainty. She seems to have been waiting for four additional factors to be right: inflation to be around 4%, unemployment continuing to fall and passing the symbolic 3 million, good local election results and consistent poll ratings around 40% for the government. By early May all these things had happened, and polling day was set for 11 June, the second successive June election.

The campaign

Although its effect on the eventual outcome was perhaps even less than usual, this was in many ways an interesting campaign.

Some things had not changed a great deal. Most of the campaign was designed for television, with public occasions and news conferences timed to suit news bulletins, and rallies restricted to the party faithful to provide good coverage. There is even a story, possibly apocryphal, that one experienced politician remained largely dormant for most of an early evening programme but then took control of proceedings for the last few minutes to impress people who were switching on early for a soap opera. Some arguments were even *about* television involvement such as the row between Anne Diamond and Denis Healey about private health and the complaints when children at a Kent primary school were given badges and hats to greet Mrs Thatcher at a "photo-opportunity". One unwelcome development was the growth of the sort of "dirty tricks" and personal attacks which had been seen in one or two earlier by-elections and which had led the Conservative agent in Truro to resign in disgust. Neil Kinnock termed it a "pretty mucky" campaign, and David Steel was awarded substantial damages when a tabloid newspaper alleged an affair with a friend's wife.

It has been generally agreed by uncommitted observers that if the outcome had been decided on the effectiveness of the campaign, Labour would have won by a street. After 1983 there was not only a new leader, there was a new team to run the next electoral campaign. Bryan Gould, Peter Mandelson and Larry Whitty were in control of things to an extent which Labour had not enjoyed for years, and were prepared to learn not only from Labour's weaknesses in 1983 but from Conservative strengths. As well as the attention given to television, care was taken to ensure that all the main figures knew what they had to do, and potentially disruptive figures and issues, such as the proposal to reimburse surcharged local councillors and striking miners were quietly marginalised. In this strategy Neil Kinnock was a great asset. Unlike several previous Labour leaders he positively enjoyed campaigning, and could respond to a live audience in a way which seemed almost to have died out, though he was never able to conquer a tendency to let his flow of words run away with him. Another Labour achievement was to make Party Election

Broadcasts interesting again. The most famous, focusing on Kinnock as a personality to a background of Brahms on a synthesiser, was scripted and directed by the *Chariots of Fire* team of Colin Welland and Hugh Hudson, part of a policy of using popular culture such as Billy Bragg's "Red Wedge" to add to their appeal. Kinnock's personal rating rose by sixteen points immediately afterwards, and requests from party workers who did not see it the first time led to the broadcast being repeated. There was a certain amount of criticism of Labour's last broadcast, showing Mrs Thatcher as a cartoon "regular royal queen" to a soundtrack of *The Gondoliers*, but it is a sign of the care with which the Labour team ran the campaign that this negative response was monitored and discussed.

By contrast the Conservative campaign looked rather lack-lustre and clumsy at times, in spite of costing £3.6 million. They used the same advertising agents (Saatchi and Saatchi) as in 1979 and 1983, which might not have been a problem if they had not tended to rely on the same tactics as well. They were certainly knocked back on their heels by the efficiency of the Labour campaign, which they had assumed would be as inept as in 1983, and by the savage questions aimed at Conservative politicians on phone-in programmes. The lack of co-ordination showed up in such disagreements as that between Mrs Thatcher and Kenneth Baker over possible fee-paying in state schools. The worst point for the Conservatives came when polls on 2 and 4 June showed a lead of only 4%–5%, and raised the possibility of a hung Parliament, something at least one Sunday newspaper had recommended. What was already a fairly fraught atmosphere at Central Office became almost panic-stricken according to some accounts, and a rescue team of Lord Young and two of Mrs Thatcher's most trusted campaign managers Tim Bell and Gordon Reece was drafted in. It is still a matter of dispute how necessary all this was. Something very similar had happened at the same point in the 1979 campaign, and the worst poll, in the *Daily Telegraph* of 4 June, was conducted by Gallup, who consistently underestimated Tory support, as they had done in 1979. One account which claims to be based on inside information implies that Young, Bell and Reece were always part of the campaign strategy, and Norman Tebbit, who as Party Chairman was responsible for campaign management, afterwards said that there was no need to pick over the bones of the campaign because there had been no corpse in the first place. The only point at which the Tory campaign looked as effective as Labour's or as their own efforts in 1983 was when their final Party Election Broadcast concentrated on Mrs Thatcher's achievements without commentary. This emphasised her stature as a world leader, something reinforced by a flying visit during the campaign to the economic summit in Venice. She had done the same in 1983 with the Williamsburg summit, which may help to explain the attraction of June elections. Though Labour dismissed the whole thing as an extended photo-opportunity, the respect accorded to Mrs Thatcher and the general endorsement of "Thatcherite" economic policies, especially President Reagan's unqualified support, contrasted sharply with Neil Kinnock's comparatively unsuccessful visits to the United States some time earlier.

The Alliance never really recovered from a number of setbacks. The publication of their manifesto, entitled "A Great Reform Charter" a day earlier than the other parties' merely led to its being swamped, and their policy of dual leadership led to tensions and at times made them look faintly ridiculous. Their retinue of two "battle buses" led to televised conversations along the lines "See you in Cardiff, or is it Nottingham?", and news conferences against a yellow backdrop at which one spoke while the other sat trying to look involved were derided by Neil Kinnock and others. The major disagreement between the two leaders, at least at this stage, concerned what would happen if there were a hung Parliament: the Liberals seemed to favour a link with Labour, Owen with the Conservatives, though not if Mrs Thatcher remained leader. The Alliance defence disagreement meant that they were unable to remain aloof from the two-party battle as they had done in 1974 and 1983. Owen's frequently expressed view at the beginning of the campaign that Labour was unelectable and that Alliance strategy should therefore be directed against the Conservatives was a mistake, in view of Labour's recovery of morale and efficiency, but was never re-thought. Most serious was the realisation by the electorate that voting for the Alliance would not only be wasted, 37% recognising that they could not win, but could let in the party they opposed. Thus as polling day approached the Alliance made increasingly desperate claims of a surge in support, whereas unlike other General Elections third-party support actually declined, whilst Labour pulled further ahead.

The result

The turnout was higher than in 1983 at 75.5%, slightly more than the average 1970–1987, but this may have been the result of giving holiday-makers a postal vote: postal votes were up by one-third. The same legislation had raised the deposit from £150, which it had been since 1918, to £500, which deterred a lot of candidates (the National Front opted out altogether) but lowered the level for the return of the deposit to 5%, which meant that only one Liberal of the three major parties lost a deposit.

The BBC's final poll, conducted by Gallup, suggested that the overall majority would only be twenty-six, which with the 3% margin of error of all opinion polls could have meant a hung Parliament. This was at odds with all the other polls over the last week, and early results gave no sign that anything of the sort was likely. The government in fact passed the necessary 326 in the early hours of 12 June, ironically at the same time as Neil Kinnock scored a resounding victory in his own constituency. After the alarms and excursions of the campaign the Conservatives were probably relieved to have 376 (including the Speaker) a net loss of 21, and an overall majority of 101 though it was a set-back to have no seats in the cities of Manchester, Liverpool or Glasgow. Their share of the vote, 42.3%, was virtually the same as in 1983 in percentage terms, but 700,000 more. Perhaps most re-assuring was that their share of C1 and C2 votes remained steady; the most worrying the loss of 4.4% of their vote in

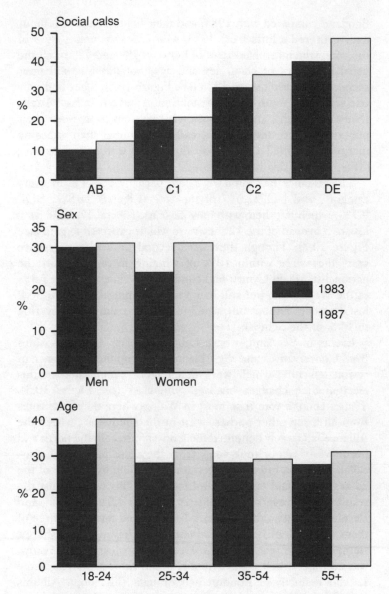

Fig. 10.1   Increase in Labour Party support, 1983–1987

Scotland compared with 1983, and their fall to 10 seats. Labour had recovered a little from 1983, with 229 seats and 30.8% of the vote, which involved rises of between 1% and 7% in all the usual categories of class, sex and age, but this was still their second worst result since 1923 (see Figure 10.1). They had only one seat in the south-west (Bristol South) and one in East Anglia (Norwich South), and most of their rise went to increase their majorities where they were already large rather than attacking marginals: in 1983 Labour had three seats with majorities over 50%, in 1987 this had risen to 22.

The Alliance had similarly fallen back by 1%–4% in every category, and had 22.6% of the vote (Liberals 12.8%, SDP 9.7%) which left them with only 22 seats (Liberal 17, SDP 5), a loss of 3 instead of the 12 they were widely expected to gain (see Figure 10.2). Though they were second in 278 Conservative seats they were within 10% of winning in only 27. Of the nationalists, Plaid Cymru had continued to slide, down to 7.3% of the Welsh vote, but still had 3 seats, gaining 1, and the SNP lost 2 seats to Labour but won 3 from Conservatives, recovering to 14% of the Scottish vote.

Events in Scotland, where Labour and the SNP took votes from Conservatives and the Alliance, point up the importance of regional factors, which were much more complicated in this election than changes involved with class (see Figure 10.3). Thus Labour's vote rose most in Wales, where they took votes from all three other parties, least in the south-east, where the Alliance fall largely benefited the Conservatives; in the north and north-west Labour took votes from the other parties. The so-called "London effect" showed Labour failing to win any of the 23 seats they had targeted, and losing 3. This was not just the result of controversial candidates such as Diane Abbott and Bernie Grant (two of four black MPs elected this time, three of them in London) because Labour's vote fell in Peter Shore's Bethnal Green seat, and Eric Deakin, who lost Walthamstow, was convinced that a 62% rate rise and the activities of some Labour councils in London had brought this about. All this shows that where people live has some effect on how they vote:

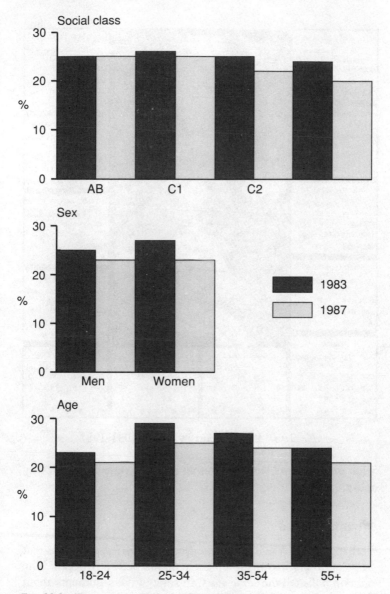

Fig. 10.2 Decrease in Liberal/SDP Alliance support, 1983–1987

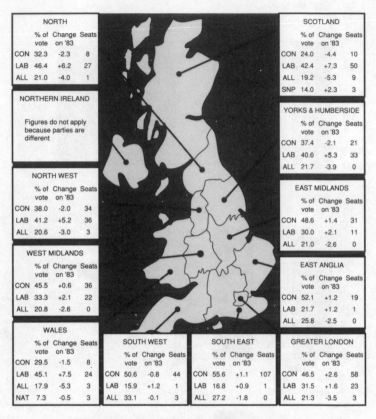

NORTH

	% of vote	Change on '83	Seats
CON	32.3	-2.3	8
LAB	46.4	+6.2	27
ALL	21.0	-4.0	1

NORTHERN IRELAND

Figures do not apply because parties are different

NORTH WEST

	% of vote	Change on '83	Seats
CON	38.0	-2.0	34
LAB	41.2	+5.2	36
ALL	20.6	-3.0	3

WEST MIDLANDS

	% of vote	Change on '83	Seats
CON	45.5	+0.6	36
LAB	33.3	+2.1	22
ALL	20.8	-2.6	0

WALES

	% of vote	Change on '83	Seats
CON	29.5	-1.5	8
LAB	45.1	+7.5	24
ALL	17.9	-5.3	3
NAT	7.3	-0.5	3

SCOTLAND

	% of vote	Change on '83	Seats
CON	24.0	-4.4	10
LAB	42.4	+7.3	50
ALL	19.2	-5.3	9
SNP	14.0	+2.3	3

YORKS & HUMBERSIDE

	% of vote	Change on '83	Seats
CON	37.4	-2.1	21
LAB	40.6	+5.3	33
ALL	21.7	-3.9	0

EAST MIDLANDS

	% of vote	Change on '83	Seats
CON	48.6	+1.4	31
LAB	30.0	+2.1	11
ALL	21.0	-2.6	0

EAST ANGLIA

	% of vote	Change on '83	Seats
CON	52.1	+1.2	19
LAB	21.7	+1.2	1
ALL	25.8	-2.5	0

SOUTH WEST

	% of vote	Change on '83	Seats
CON	50.6	-0.8	44
LAB	15.9	+1.2	1
ALL	33.1	-0.1	3

SOUTH EAST

	% of vote	Change on '83	Seats
CON	55.6	+1.1	107
LAB	16.8	+0.9	1
ALL	27.2	-1.8	0

GREATER LONDON

	% of vote	Change on '83	Seats
CON	46.5	+2.6	58
LAB	31.5	+1.6	23
ALL	21.3	-3.5	3

Fig. 10.3 Party support by region, 1983–1987

what we do not yet know is whether people's votes change if they move.

What happened?

Perhaps the most telling statistic from the 1987 campaign is that 81% of voters had made up their minds before it began. The opinion polls tell the same story, in spite of the arguments about their reliability, as Table 10.1 shows. Thus the success of the

Table 10.1 *Opinion polls during the 1987 General Election campaign.*

(Percentages)			
Start of campaign		*Highest/lowest*	*Result*
Conservative	44	45–39	42.3
Labour	33	36.5–28	30.8
Alliance	21	26–18	22.6

Labour campaign and the traumas of "Wobbly Thursday" for the Conservatives had made no real difference to the outcome.

In one sense this is surprising, particularly to those analysts who believe that voters now make up their minds on the issues: at least 75% of the electorate saw health, unemployment and education as the three most important issues, and Labour were ahead of the Conservatives on these by 12%–27%. The most plausible explanation is a combination of policy and the electorate's confidence, what might be termed "perceived competence": put crudely, whether a party had plans which the voters liked, and was believed to have the capacity to put them into practice. In the case of the Alliance, perceived competence was the major factor, since they found it very difficult to project policies that differed from what the other parties were offering. As early as May 1986 one analyst was pointing out that to be a plausible governing party they would have to do more than proclaim what they were against. The disagreements before and during the campaign had suggested that they were unlikely to be able to "get it together", and as the novelty had worn off they had become less attractive to the media.

Confidence was part of the story with Labour. Although Neil Kinnock was superficially attractive, 44% believed that he would make the worst Prime Minister, as against 31% believing he would be the best: one analyst unkindly described his popularity as consisting principally of not being Michael Foot. Important though this sort of image can be, as the Party Election Broadcasts tried to promote, policies also played a major part. Labour were still vulnerable on defence. Kinnock has been a supporter of CND since his student days, and the Labour Party Conference had passed by a majority of five to one a motion calling for Polaris to be scrapped "from day one". The electorate did not like this to judge from the polls: 75% believed that the United Kingdom should keep an independent nuclear deterrent, and the Conservatives were 21% ahead of Labour on this. They were also uncertain on the cost of their programme, and John MacGregor was able to claim for the Conservatives that VAT would have to rise to 41% from its current level of 15% to pay for everything Labour was proposing, a claim they were never really able to refute convincingly. Labour were also committed to clawing back the 2p tax cut from the 1987 budget, and those earning over £27,000 would lose all the tax concessions they had gained since 1979. Understandably those who felt wealthier under the Conservatives were reluctant to risk becoming poorer under Labour.

By contrast, the Conservatives seemed the most likely to maintain the overall mood of greater prosperity, something which has aptly become known as "pocket-book" voting. The creation of a new prosperous working class is considered elsewhere in the book, but there is little doubt that the fall in inflation, the cuts in direct taxation and the creation of a whole new class of shareholders through the privatisation programme had given rise to a mood where a very high proportion of voters not only felt but were better off, and regarded the Conservatives not only as responsible for this condition so far, but as the party most likely to maintain it beyond the election.

11

The General Election of 1992

According to legend, Sir Robin Day said of the 1987 General Election that there had been absolutely no change on the political scene, and therefore the whole thing had been a total waste of time. It did not take very long for the changes to begin, and by the end of 1990 the political landscape had taken on a very different appearance.

The first changes took place in the Alliance of Liberals and Social Democrats. It was clear that the electorate had not responded favourably to two parties trying to co-operate while retaining their own identities, policies and leadership, and that something more definite was needed if they were to become a realistic alternative to Labour, let alone the Conservatives. Within days of the election David Steel proposed that the two parties should merge, something which was happening at local level anyway in many parts of the country. For a time it looked as though merging two parties was going to produce three, with opposition from hard-line Liberals who echoed Sir Cyril Smith's view that the Alliance should have been strangled at birth, as well as from three SDP MPs, the leader David Owen, Rosie Barnes and John Cartwright. The other two SDP MPs, Charles Kennedy and Robert Maclennan supported merger, as did a majority of the rank and file. In August 1988 the process of change was completed when Paddy Ashdown was elected leader of the new party to replace David Steel, and after several attempts to hit on a name which reflected its dual origins, they settled on Liberal Democrats. In spite of David Owen's undoubted charisma and the organisational skills of John Cartwright the SDP found it impossible to survive. Apart from a near-success at Richmond in February 1989 (taking 32.2% of the vote to 37.2 for the Conservatives) their by-election support fell steadily until at Bootle on 24 May 1990 their candidate suffered the indignity of scoring fewer votes than "Screaming Lord" Sutch: for the record Sutch gained 418 votes, the SDP candidate 155, compared with 6,820 in the 1987 General Election. Politicians can survive most things, but looking ridiculous is almost always terminal, and it was no surprise that the SDP was wound up barely a week after the Bootle result.

As outlined in the previous chapter, the Conservatives were anxious to avoid the impression that they had run out of ideas after two terms in office. The problem was that many of their initiatives proved extremely unpopular. Of these the most spectacular failure was the attempt to find a replacement for domestic rates as a means of raising part of local government revenue. This had been in the 1979 manifesto, the only part of that programme not to be implemented by 1983, but there were serious objections to every possible alternative. The choice eventually fell on the "community charge", soon dubbed the poll tax, a flat-rate payment by all adults. There were numerous arguments in favour: it would do away with the anomaly that the same amount was payable whether there was one wage-earner or several in a property; it would be less costly to individuals than the rates, in theory; and it would increase the accountability of local authorities, since if more people were paying, they would have an incentive to vote out councils which overspent. The main disadvantage in principle was that couples and families would be worse off in total; the main problem in practice was that its implementation was a classic case of how not to do it. There was a great deal of anguished dithering over whether to phase the charge or introduce it in one go, and the decision to introduce the charge a year early into Scotland to avoid a rate revaluation merely enabled the opposition to become even better organised. The Anti-Poll Tax Union staged some of the biggest demonstrations seen in London and elsewhere for many years, and news programmes were dominated by stories of people refusing to pay. Beside this, other issues were less controversial, but there was widespread apprehension about changes in the National Health Service, especially the proposal that hospitals could become self-governing trusts and GPs take greater responsibility for their own budgets.

These issues had a great effect on the government's fortunes in by-elections. After narrowly holding Richmond, though with their greatest loss of support compared with the General Election (24.1%), they did not hold another seat before the General Election. The loss of Eastbourne to the Liberals in October 1990 was clearly the result of resentment at the poll tax, and in Monmouth (May 1991) there was great concern at the future of the local hospital: the government's claims that they had been misunderstood and misrepresented made little difference.

As well as losing seats, comparatively unimportant with such a large majority, the government was also losing key figures, and this was much more damaging, highlighting the other two issues on which they were vulnerable, the economy and Europe. Following "Black Monday" (19 October 1987) when the Stock Market fell 15%, Nigel Lawson, the Chancellor of the Exchequer, made two key decisions: to continue to reflate the economy, building on the 1986 and 1987 Budgets, and to link the pound more closely to the Deutschmark. Instead of saving, people spent, and the rise in inflation and in the balance of payments deficit caused a massive rise in interest rates, from 7½% in May 1988 to 13% in November, with inevitable consequences for mortgage rates and investment, leading to a renewed rise in unemployment. Lawson had been anxious to join the Exchange Rate Mechanism, but Mrs Thatcher was not keen, and her apparent readiness to listen to her economic adviser Sir Alan Walters, who regarded the ERM as "half-baked" led to Lawson's resignation in October 1989. In July 1990 Nicholas Ridley resigned after some undiplomatic remarks about Germany in a magazine interview (ironically in a journal edited by Lawson's son Dominic), but the most damaging departure was that of Sir Geoffrey Howe in November of the same year. In a resignation speech of extraordinary savagery, particularly coming from someone described by Ridley as "careful, thorough and lugubrious", and who had seemed to accept everything Mrs Thatcher chose to do to him he made clear his frustration with Mrs Thatcher's style in general and her attitude to Europe in particular. Mrs Thatcher had managed to fend off a challenge to her leadership in 1989 from Sir Anthony Meyer, but the events of 1990 provided a spring-board for a much more serious attempt by Michael Heseltine, who had been aloof from the government's problems since his resignation at the beginning of 1986 and who opposed the poll tax. Under the Conservatives' Byzantine rules for leadership elections Mrs Thatcher fell four votes short of winning on the first ballot. She was in France at a European Summit, and rushed out to announce "I fight on, I fight to win". For many this was the last straw, since she had not consulted any of her Cabinet colleagues before deciding to go on. The unthinkable happened: most of her Cabinet told her that if she remained as leader the Conservatives would lose the next election, and she should therefore withdraw before the second ballot. On 27 November John Major, the 47-year-old Chancellor of the Exchequer, secured the largest share of the vote, comfortably beating Heseltine and Douglas Hurd: they withdrew, and the Chairman of the 1922 Committee announced that there would be no third ballot, whatever the rules might say.

Meanwhile Labour had been quietly rebuilding. They had recognised that the changes in Labour's policies and presentation had not been enough to attract the electorate, and that they needed something much more radical, especially in the fields of defence and the economy. The unilateralist stance of 1983 and 1987 was dropped, a market economy was tacitly accepted, as was the impossibility of reversing most of the government's privatisations, and a start was made on reversing some of the more damaging changes of the early 1980s. Left-wingers complained that they had been stifled, and Tony Benn lamented the end of Labour as a party of debate, but in taking the party much closer to a Social Democrat position Neil Kinnock enjoyed

"There's a 10p fine every time you say 'It's the end of an era'."

© The Daily Telegraph

a domination over the party conferences in 1989 and 1990 unprecedented when Labour has been in opposition, and unusual at any time. The growing success of Labour in making themselves electable was confirmed by opinion polls: in 1990 before Mrs Thatcher's fall Labour were between 9 and 24 points ahead of the Conservatives. In every by-election between June 1989 and November 1990 Labour saw their share of the vote increase, most spectacularly in Mid-Staffordshire in March 1990 where they took the seat from the Conservatives with more than double their General Election showing.

Although the replacement of Mrs Thatcher by John Major was in many ways tantamount to a change of government, it did not lead to a radical change of fortune. There was a brief honeymoon period (in October 1990 the Conservatives trailed by 34% to 45%: in November they led by 46% to 39%), but it did not last, and the catalogue of by-election losses went on, including Ribble Valley, their tenth safest seat in England, in March 1991. The economy was still in crisis, and the Gulf War with Iraq failed to provide any sort of "Falklands Factor": although Kuwait was liberated, Saddam Hussein remained in power, and there was widespread horror at the plight of Kurdish refugees.

The question of the next General Election began with the election of John Major, though there is no constitutional reason for a new Prime Minister to go to the country immediately: Eden was probably the last to call an election almost immediately after becoming Prime Minister. From force of habit election-watchers began to expect something to happen from June 1991, but John Major was anxious to see the economy show clear signs of recovery and resisted the temptation to call the election for November to capitalise on the end of the Gulf War. On the other hand he did not want to get pushed into a corner, as had happened most notably with James Callaghan in 1979. The Budget came earlier than usual, on 10 March 1992, and though it was not received with notable enthusiasm, it signalled an April election and polling day was set for 9 April.

The campaign

The Conservatives were behind in all but one of the opinion polls taken within two days of the announcement on 11 March, the first time since 1979 that a government had gone into a General Election without a lead, and the first time since 1974 that the Conservatives had been in that position. The style of the various campaigns reflected the mood of the parties: Labour confident and professional, building on their successful strategy of 1987; the Conservatives defensive and muddled; and the Liberals concerned with the problems and opportunities of holding the balance.

Unfortunately for the majority of the electorate most of the campaign was extremely tedious. Most of the arguments had been rehearsed many times over the previous months, and there was a sense that the processes of election management were more important than the people or the policies, with much of the attention being focused on the nature of the campaign rather than its objects. This led many observers to complain that the most important issues were never considered, a point discussed further in later chapters. When such matters as voting reform were discussed it was more as a bargaining counter in forming a hypothetical coalition than for any merits or significance it might possess as a constitutional reform. The 1992 campaign finally killed off the textbook belief that great questions are decided by General Elections.

During the first week of the campaign the economic news on output and inflation was bad, allowing Labour to attack with their "alternative budget", and overshadowing the Liberal manifesto. The majority of the polls had Labour at least 2% ahead, with the Liberals on 18%, reinforcing the possibility of a hung parliament, but the Conservatives seemed relieved that it was no worse. In the second week Labour tried to shift the debate to the National Health Service and the impact of underfunding with an election broadcast focusing on the plight of a little girl suffering from "glue ear". It was somehow typical that the key point got lost in a welter of accusations and counter-accusations when "Jennifer" was identified to the press, and it became known that one of her parents had written to the Conservatives and the other to Labour. Both major parties suffered as those surveyed expressed their impatience with sterile point-scoring, and the only party to benefit was the Liberals: John Major's rating fell, Neil Kinnock's remained steady but Paddy Ashdown's soared.

In 1979 and 1987 the Conservatives had suffered their worst phase of the campaign a week before polling day. In 1992 this came early and in an apparently far worse form. At the start of the third week of the campaign two polls (Harris for ITN and MORI in *The Times*) put Labour at least 6% ahead, with the Conservatives on 35%, the worst for any government since the war. Labour were encouraged to think that they might secure an overall majority and form a government without the need to rely on any other party. This mood was seen at its strongest in the rally which Labour held on 1 April in Sheffield, when the members of the Shadow Cabinet were introduced as ministers.

In a later interview Neil Kinnock said that he had not intended this, nor the whoops of triumph which he gave when he reached the rostrum, but was buoyed up by the reception. How much difference this made is arguable: prominent Labour figures have since described it as a distraction from what they should have been doing rather than a decisive contribution to the eventual result. At least parties may have been put off tempting providence in that way in the future by the outcome in 1992.

In policy terms, constitutional issues began to figure more prominently. Labour invited other parties to join them in talks on reform once the election was over, and Paddy Ashdown threatened to vote down any Queen's Speech which did not contain a specific commitment to reform of the voting system. John Major decisively rejected all talk of electoral reform or of independence for Scotland, though he did promise to "take stock" of the Scottish situation. As the campaign drew to a close Labour returned to the NHS as their major issue, while the Conservatives concentrated on their perceived strengths of prices and taxation, and the Liberals continued to emphasise their conditions for support in a hung parliament. Polls suggested that the electorate did not find this an appealing prospect: 57% disapproved of a hung parliament, and 42% opposed electoral reform, compared with 39% in favour.

By polling day the opinion polls were broadly agreed that the parties were virtually together: Gallup in the *Daily Telegraph* had the Conservatives on 38.5%, Labour 38% and the Liberals 20%, while the ICM poll in the *Guardian* had the two parties locked on 38%. This was not greatly different from the situation at the start, whatever the intervening fluctuations might have

The Daily Telegraph

ESTABLISHED 1855 · NO. 42,567   45p

LONDON AND MANCHESTER

THURSDAY, APRIL 9, 1992

Polls put parties neck and neck

been, and confirmed David Butler's observation that this was the first General Election for a long time in which a hung parliament and its consequences had been on the agenda from the start. The Conservatives had made up a great deal of ground since the low point of 31 March, but it remained an open question whether they had done enough even to be the largest party.

The result

The 1992 election set a number of records. Forty-three million were entitled to vote, half a million of them for the first time: since the turnout was the highest since February 1974, at 77.7%, this meant that there was a record number of voters, as well as a record number of candidates, nearly 2,948 compared with 2,325 in 1987. The indications that the Conservatives had been making up ground in the latter stages of the campaign were confirmed by the television exit polls. ITN gave the Conservatives 41%, Labour 37% and the Liberals 18%, while the BBC had the Conservatives on 42%, Labour 36% and the Liberals 18%. This implied that Labour had still not done quite enough, and this was confirmed by the early results, which showed Labour failing to take the seats they needed to become the largest party. The most significant was Basildon, natural habitat of "Essex Man": with its small majority after 1987 and a Labour-controlled council it was a seat Labour had to win. It was one of the first to declare, and though there was a swing of 1.3% from Conservative to Labour that still left David Amess with a majority of 1,480. Rather like Salford in 1970, Basildon showed the trend for the rest of the results; though there were swings to Labour, they were not enough either in scale or consistency. For some reason the BBC had decided to revive its Swingometer in a new and more elaborate form, with symbols that changed colour as the pointer moved. The swings were so erratic that it was impossible to generalise. Not only were there major variations from one region to another, they occurred even within a region: Folkestone and Hythe saw a swing of 0.6% from Conservative to Liberal, while the next-door constituency of

Dover saw a swing of 5.2% from Conservative to Labour. Devizes set some sort of record by registering no swing in any direction. The margin of victory between Conservative and Labour was 7.5%, the third largest post-war and beaten only by the margins of 1983 and 1987, but this was not reflected in seats, with Labour doing better than their share of the vote would have produced if the "Cube Law" had been operating, as discussed in Chapter 1. The Conservatives passed the 326 mark at lunch-time on Friday 10 April, and the final result was: Conservatives 336 (41.9%); Labour 271 (34.4%); Liberals 20 (17.8%); Scottish National Party 3; Plaid Cymru 4; Others (Northern Ireland) 17. Thus the Conservatives had a majority of only 21 in a House of Commons increased to 651 by the division of Milton Keynes into two seats, both won by Conservatives.

The implications of the 1992 election for the various national parties are discussed in the appropriate chapters, but the variations in swing were particularly apparent in Scotland. In the last group of by-elections, on 7 November 1991, the Conservatives had lost Kincardine and Deeside, seeing their majority of 2,063 turned into a Liberal majority of 7,824 on a swing of 11.4%, and this was expected to herald a further collapse, and the possible extinction of the Tories in Scotland. Instead their share of the vote rose to 25.7% (still their third worst showing, with only October 1974 and 1987 showing a lower figure) and they regained the seats lost in by-elections, as they did in the whole of Britain. The SNP rose to 21.5%, their best showing since 1974, but they were bitterly disappointed to lose Govan, won so spectacularly at the height of the poll tax campaign in Scotland. Labour's vote had fallen from 42.4% to 39%, and the Liberals had lost 6.1% of the Alliance vote in 1987 to record only 13%.

In some ways the result was disappointing for the Liberals in general. They had held 20 seats, but had lost a significant share of the vote compared with the Alliance, and had lost every seat won in a by-election since 1987, of which the loss of Eastbourne was especially galling. The victory at Bath, unseating the Party Chairman Chris Patten, was only slight compensation. The Liberals won three other seats from the Conservatives, but the

Tories won two from the Liberals as well as regaining all the by-election losses. The Liberals also lost a seat to Plaid Cymru.

One oddity of this election had been the arrival of the Natural Law Party, who fielded over 300 candidates backed by followers of the Beatles' former "guru" the Maharishi Mahesh Yogi. Their aims were not clear, except a demand for lower taxes for everybody, and they failed to make any impact on the outcome, scoring only a handful of votes and coming last in virtually every seat they fought. At least they provided a reminder that every citizen has the right to stand for Parliament.

What happened?

Two groups in particular were asking this: as in 1970 it was the Labour Party and the pollsters. The underlying problems for Labour are discussed in Chapter 13, but there were a number of factors which they were inclined to blame in the immediate aftermath. Many constituency parties and prominent Labour figures were highly critical of Labour's campaign for "substituting show-business for socialism", and others complained that Labour had "taken their eye off the ball" in getting bogged down in arguments about constitutional reform rather than concentrating on those issues where they were strongest. Yet another explanation is summed up in the headline "It's the Sun wot won it", the claim that the Conservative recovery and Labour decline was mainly caused by the impact of tabloid newspapers. This view was given support by Lord McAlpine, a former Treasurer of the Conservative Party, but this was much more a criticism of the unsteady campaign devised by "Patten's pups", as the predominantly young and inexperienced team at Central Office were known. In fact only 45% of *Sun* readers voted Conservative, as against 36% voting Labour and 14% Liberal. The poll tax was also brought in to explain Labour's showing: some left-wingers argued that many Labour supporters had failed to register to vote in order to avoid paying. The evidence is inconclusive, but there does not seem to be a clear correlation between high levels of poll tax, high numbers of unregistered "voters" and low Labour turnout. The pollsters were appalled that they had been so far out in all their predictions, since they thought they had ironed out such problems after 1970, and even more concerned that they might have been overestimating Labour support all along. The answer to the queries of both Labour and the pollsters lies in two sets of information: the stage at which voters firmly decided how to vote (Table 11.1), and the issues on which they made up their minds.

Table 11.1 *Voting decision*

	Long ago	*Start of campaign*	*Last few days*
1983	78	14	8
1987	81	12	7
1992	73	13	14

Thus over a quarter of voters had not made up their minds by 10 March, in spite of the long period of anticipation, and over half of those left the decision until the last minute: there are even stories of voters going into the polling booth intending to vote one way, and then changing when they came to put a cross. The Conservatives were the main beneficiaries of this. According to the Newsnight survey, of those who decided in the last few days, 11% of those intending to vote Liberal voted Conservative; 4% of those intending to vote Labour voted Conservative; and 8% of those intending to vote Labour voted Liberal. It seems that Conservative voters were more likely than others to conceal their intentions from the pollsters.

For much of the time the Conservative campaign appeared to consist of ministers unveiling a succession of posters. One of these showed two boxing gloves labelled "More Taxes" and "Higher Prices", dubbed "Labour's Double Whammy". Evidence shows that these were the issues which gave the Conservatives the most help, as their lead on those increased sharply during the campaign, most of it in the last few days. By contrast Labour lost ground on their strongest issues (Table 11.2). The priorities of voters are well summarised by the anonymous voter in Battersea quoted in Edward Pearce's *Election Rides*

Table 11.2   *Party strength on issues (lead over other party)*

	Start of campaign	Polling day	Change
Conservative			
Inflation	+14	+29	+15
Taxation	+10	+20	+10
Europe	+27	+35	+8
Law and Order	+16	+22	+6
Defence	+35	+41	+6
Labour			
Health	+26	+17	−9
Education	+12	+6	−6
Unemployment	+22	+16	−6
Homelessness	+28	+25	−3

Source: Gallup figures from the *Daily Telegraph*.

who was *concerned* about the environment and *wanted* lower taxes (my italics).

Labour also lost ground on leadership, as in 1987. In that election Neil Kinnock had trailed Mrs Thatcher by 31% to 42% as the best Prime Minister, and 44% believed Kinnock would be the worst, giving him a negative rating of 13%. Table 11.3 shows the fortunes of the leaders in 1992. The proportion regarding Kinnock as the worst PM was 51%, giving him a negative rating of 30%, the worst for any post-war party leader. John Major was clearly a positive asset to his party in the campaign, particularly once he managed to shake off his image-makers and revert to the sort of campaigning he preferred. His manifest sincerity, especially in his last election broadcast, and

Table 11.3   *Image of party leaders*

	Start of campaign	7/8 April	Polling day
Major	41%	39%	47%
Kinnock	25%	28%	21%
Ashdown	21%	18%	17%

his readiness to come out decisively against electoral reform or devolution as prices worth paying to hang on to power paid dividends, and like Edward Heath he was almost the only one to believe that he would win when most indications were that he would lose. The only question was whether his qualities would prove to be enough when the government had the smallest majority for the Conservatives since 1951.

12
The Conservative Party

As a party of government the Conservatives have dominated the period 1945 to 1992 (Figure. 12.1). By the time of the next General Election in 1996 or 1997 they will have been in office for two-thirds of the period, including one period of 13 years and one of 17 or 18. There is therefore some justification for their belief that they should always be in office, and that their periods of opposition merely represent temporary aberrations on the part of the electorate before an inevitable return to power.

Only in the uncertain years of the 1970s did their support fall significantly below 40% of those voting. The Conservatives had begun the 1970s with a victory that was largely unexpected, and which gave them a share of the vote, 46.4%, which was their fourth highest of the post-war period and a level not attained since. This did not last: as already described they suffered a number of problems, some of them of their own making. Though they entered the General Election campaign in February 1974 only about 2% below their 1970 share, they lost steadily during the campaign to finish at 37.8%, their lowest up to then. Things got worse in October, when their share fell by a further 2%, representing a loss of 1.4 million votes during those few months.

This led to a period in which analysts began to ask whether the Conservatives could ever win again, whether the "pendulum" (Chapter 1) had got stuck. Work done at Essex University had suggested that the natural level of support for the Conservatives was in the range 42%-44%. Whenever the Conservatives had

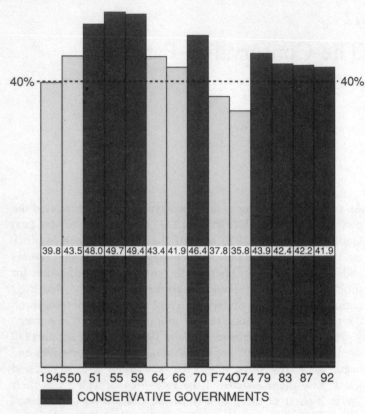

39.8	43.5	48.0	49.7	49.4	43.4	41.9	46.4	37.8	35.8	43.9	42.4	42.2	41.9

1945 50   51   55   59   64   66   70 F74 O74 79   83   87   92

■ CONSERVATIVE GOVERNMENTS

Fig. 12.1   Conservative vote-share, 1945–1992

been at that level or below, as in 1950, 1964 or 1966 they had lost, in the last by nearly 100 seats. Since the conclusions have been undermined by subsequent results there is no need to go into detail here, but they were based on the belief that Labour had gained steadily among the middle classes during the decade 1964–1974. The Conservatives would be unlikely to break down this support, and future success would depend on a higher turnout by Conservative supporters, or on short-term factors. The underlying trends of class de-alignment were operating against the Conservatives, it was believed.

The next General Election, in 1979, cast considerable doubt on this analysis: the Conservative share of the vote, 43.9%, was their lowest winning share, and their lowest of any sort since 1964. On the other hand, they had been favoured by the short-term factor of industrial relations as revealed in the Winter of Discontent. By comparison with October 1974 Conservative support among trade unionists had risen from 23% to 35%, whereas Labour had seen their trade union support fall from 55% to 50% and the Liberals from 22% to 15%. Even so, few would have predicted in 1979 that the Conservatives would win the next three General Elections with the same level of support or less, and clearly short-term factors such as the rise of centre parties or the state of the economy no longer provide a completely satisfactory explanation.

Table 12.1 *Support for the Conservatives by social class. 1964–1992*

	AB	C1	C2	DE
1964	75	61	34	31
1966	72	59	32	26
1970	79	59	35	33
Feb. 1974	67	51	30	25
Oct. 1974	63	51	26	22
1979	59		40	34
1983	60	51	40	33
1987	57	51	40	30
1992	57	49	35	29

There are many factors to explain the long series of Conservative successes. Analysis according to the familiar criteria of social class and age reveals some of the answers (Table 12.1). This suggests that after the peak of 1970, where the Conservatives recorded their highest share so far in three of the four class categories, there was a steady decline during the first half of the 1970s in all groups. The decline continued among middle-class voters: support among AB voters in 1987 and 1992 was less than three-quarters of its 1970 level, and after a stable period support

among C1 voters declined again in 1992. The difference from
1979 to 1987 was the much higher share of the vote among C2,
in 1983 and 1987 higher than Labour. The Conservatives' share
of DE voters peaked in 1979, and declined thereafter, though
in 1992 it was still higher than 1966 or 1974. This level of
support among working class voters was something which the
analysts in 1978 thought unlikely, though they conceded that
many voters did not like Labour policies.

Table 12.2   *The "new" working class, 1983–1992*

	1983		1987		1992	
	Con.	Lab.	Con.	Lab.	Con.	Lab.
Lives in south	42	26	46	28	40	38
Owner/occupier	47	25	44	32	40	41
Private sector	36	37	38	39	32	50
Non-union (1992 only)					37	46

The levels of support for the Conservatives particularly among
the skilled working class since 1979 have been explained by Ivor
Crewe's division of the working class into "old" and "new". The
new working class lives in the South, works in the private sector,
consists largely of owner-occupiers, and contains a low proportion of trade union members (Table 12.2). The moral is clear
for 1983, and to a great extent for 1987, with the Conservatives
comfortably ahead of Labour in two of the three categories, and
only just behind among private sector workers. The 1992
election, however, showed a different picture confirming trends
which had already been apparent beforehand. The implications
for Labour are considered in the next chapter, but the fact that
the Conservatives were behind in all but one category suggested
that the privatisation programme has made very little difference
to the perception of workers, indeed may have made them more
likely to vote Labour, and the impact of the very high interest
rates and low house prices (the "equity trap" whereby house-
owners have become committed to repaying far more than their
house is now worth) which prevailed for much of the period from
1987 explains the decline in owner-occupier support for the

Conservatives. Even the Conservative lead among workers in the south has been shown to be extremely vulnerable in by-elections both before and after the 1992 General Election: on the evidence of 1992 the electoral trends among the working class may no longer be operating in the way which the Conservatives had come to assume as inevitable.

Analysis by age offers a little more hope for the Conservatives, though changes in presenting the figures make exact comparisons impossible. Among the youngest voters (18–24) it was the norm for Labour to have an advantage, indeed in the two elections of 1974 they led the Conservatives by 13% and 18%, but the gap narrowed to 1% in 1979 and in 1983 the Conservatives were ahead by 9%. Though Labour regained the lead in 1987, one set of figures had the Conservatives ahead again in 1992, so that Labour can no longer assume solid support among young and first-time voters. At the other end of the age spectrum the Conservatives have consistently been around 50% among voters over 65 since 1974, whereas Labour have declined from 38% in 1979 to 31% in 1992. In the 1970s analysts suggested that this ought to worry the Conservatives as their support died off and Labour apparently secured the loyalty of the younger voters. As discussed in Chapter 17, there is now much less automatic loyalty between one election and the next, and this is particularly true of Labour supporters. In addition the birth-rate has been declining while the numbers of people living significantly beyond retirement have increased, especially as a proportion of the population as a whole. These demographic changes could represent a continuing advantage for the Conservatives, one which they need, on the evidence of the year following the 1992 General Election.

An important factor in Conservative dominance since the Second World War, and indeed throughout its history, has been the party's capacity to re-invent itself in the face of set-backs, a process which has often been carried out by an outsider. In the 1830s and 1840s Robert Peel forced the Tories to accept the implications of the Great Reform Act and the growth of European industrialisation. Disraeli developed the policy of

Imperialism as a means of attracting the support of the newly-enfranchised urban workers in the 1870s, and later Joseph Chamberlain convinced the party of the need to abandon Free Trade in favour of Imperial Preference. Following the defeat in 1945 the party came to terms with the main premises of the post-war consensus, and in the 1960s Edward Heath took the process even further. After two failures in 1974 Margaret Thatcher, with considerable inspiration from Keith Joseph, devised a radical alternative to the post-war consensus based on a combination of conviction rhetoric and laisser-faire economics, and with her departure in 1990 the party embarked on revisions of both style and content which were enough to win the 1992 election, though there has to be a question mark over the future.

One aspect of this continuous process of adaptation which is very apparent in the period since 1945 is the party's ruthlessness in respect of leaders. Every post-war leader of the Conservative party has left in circumstances of considerable controversy. Churchill did not want to go, even at the age of 80 in poor health: Eden was tainted by the failure of Suez, and his successor, Harold Macmillan was distrusted by many in the party. When Macmillan retired in 1963 there were grave doubts about the method of selection and the character of his successor, Alec Douglas-Home, whose career was ended by the defeat in 1964. Three losses in four contests were enough to see the replacement of Edward Heath by Margaret Thatcher, and she was unseated by the prospect of loss, even though she had won every election as leader. Even election success cannot guarantee survival these days.

The decline of automatic loyalty to the leader on the part of the party rank and file has been especially noticeable since the 1992 General Election, and this highlights another important factor in Conservative success: their image as the most effective party in government. In the days of relatively stable voting allegiance, the substantial number of working-class voters supporting the Conservatives was put down to "deference", the belief that they were the best equipped to rule by experience and skill. With the decline in party identification deference voting also diminished, and by the 1980s opinion polls were reflecting declining confidence on the part of the electorate about what the government was doing. This was the case in every Parliament, as already outlined in the backgrounds to 1983, 1987 and 1992, but the events of the months following the latest General Election showed the government losing support on an unprecedented scale. The most divisive issue was Europe, and Britain's involvement in its development. In the autumn of 1992 the pound fell out of the bottom of the exchange rate mechanism, which had been trumpeted as the main element in the government's counter-inflationary strategy, and ratification of the Maastricht Treaty gave Eurosceptics a specific issue on which to unite and challenge the official line. Even the successes of the Edinburgh Summit at the end of 1992 could not make Europe a positive issue for the Conservatives. The decision to close 31 pits and put 30,000 miners out of work, and the subsequent climb-down in the face of backbench revolt, the long-running dispute over testing in schools, and controversy over the sale of arms to Iraq all gave the impression of a government which had lost its way, and a Prime Minister who, for all his attractive qualities, was not really up to the job.

Table 12.3   *Party support, August–November 1992*

	(Election)	Aug.	Sept.	Oct.	Nov.
Con.	42.8	38.4	36.9	32.0	30.2
Lab.	35.2	42.6	44.5	48.4	51.5
Labour lead	−7.6	+4.2	+7.6	+16.4	+21.3

Opinion polls in the last months of 1992 showed the scale of the problem (Tables 12.3 and 12.4). Though there was a slight improvement in the early months of 1993, there was still a perceived lack of confidence, emphasised by the loss of the safe seat of Newbury to the Liberals and of control of all but one of the Conservatives' County Councils in May. Pressure from the media and from backbenchers led to the decision to remove Norman Lamont, who had been vulnerable as Chancellor since Black Wednesday in September 1992: this revived recollections of a similar action by Harold Macmillan in 1962.

Table 12.4   *Satisfaction with the Prime Minister*

	Aug.	Sept.	Oct.	Nov.
Satisfied	45.2	38.7	25.6	23.3
Dissatisfied	44.8	52.1	67.0	69.0
	(+0.4)	(−13.4)	(−41.4)	(−45.7)

Source: Gallup surveys published in the *Daily Telegraph*.

This did not work, to judge from opinion polls taken at the end of May. The Gallup "snapshot" of a thousand electors gave Labour 49% (up 2% from the previous month), Conservatives 25% (down 5%) and the Liberals 23% (up 5.5%), suggesting that the government could find itself in third place before long. The May Gallup 9000 showed a similarly gloomy picture (Table 12.5).

Table 12.5   *Gallup 9000, March–May 1993*

	March	April	May
Conservative	30.0	30.9	26.8
Labour	48.3	47.4	44.2
Liberal	15.8	16.0	23.6
Major		23.2	20.4
Smith	as best PM	31.5	30.3
Ashdown		17.5	21.6

Most serious was the decline in respect for the Conservatives' economic competence (Table 12.6). In October 1992 80% had believed that economic conditions were the worst they had ever known, and 95% expected the recession to last beyond the end of 1993. Of those in work only 56% believed their jobs to be safe. Overall Labour had a lead of 47% to 29% on the question as to which party would do the better job in running the

Table 12.6   *Economic competence, March–May 1993*

	(Election)	March	April	May
Conservative	44.6	26.9	28.1	27.1
Labour	38.0	40.5	40.8	40.5

economy. In spite of improvements in output and (somewhat surprisingly) in unemployment in the spring of 1993 the electorate was still unconvinced. Under 20% expected things to get better, against 34% who expected them to get worse. About the only consolation, as in similar straits in the 1980s, was that there was still a long time to go before another General Election.

There were several differences, however. In the first place, there was a very different style of leadership. At first this had come as something of a relief after the increasingly strident dogmatism of Mrs Thatcher's last years, but after the 1992 General Election there was an apparent inability to deal with the most serious issues. This is a problem which other Conservative leaders have found in replacing a long-serving and dynamic figure, such as Eden after Churchill and Douglas-Home following Macmillan. Image has been important to the Conservatives throughout the post-war period, and they are well aware that the image of the leader and that of the party are inextricably intertwined. The dumping of Mrs Thatcher is only the most recent example of the readiness of the Conservatives to change the leader as a means of changing the party's image and fortunes: "autocracy tempered by the legal right of revolution", to adapt Theodore Mommsen's phrase. Although only 15% of voters had any confidence in John Major by the summer of 1993, making him the most unpopular Prime Minister since Gallup began asking the question in 1938, and below even the level reached by Mrs Thatcher in the summer of 1990 none of the alternatives had any more support: 42% answered "Don't know" to the question "Who would make the best Prime Minister?", implying a lack of real quality in the Conservative party as a whole.

Another problem faced by the Conservatives which had not been a problem for Mrs Thatcher was the size of the majority, 21 after the General Election, cut to 19 by the Newbury defeat and likely to fall still further, especially if by-elections occurred in the heartlands of the Tory south. Backbenchers re-discovered their power, and forced significant concessions on such key areas of policy as rail privatisation. If a government backs down too often it risks looking even more indecisive, but demands for unity and loyalty met with little response from people who were enjoying the chance to have a significant impact on government, which is good for democracy, but less helpful to a party's chances of winning the next election.

The final handicap for the Conservatives was that the Liberals had recovered from the traumas of the late 1980s and were proving the same refuge for protesting Tories that they had been in the 1960s and 1970s. The result at Newbury, where the swing from Conservatives to Liberals was over 28%, the largest since 1973 and one of the largest post-war was confirmed by the county council results on the same day. More recent opinion polls suggested that Liberal strength was continuing to grow especially in the south-west: if the trends indicated by the May 1993 polls were to be reproduced in the next General Election, then the whole area from Hampshire to Cornwall would be Liberal with the possible exception of some Labour success in Exeter and Plymouth. It has been scant consolation that the Conservatives in 1992 won back every seat lost since 1987: that recovery looked unlikely to be repeated on the evidence of the summer of 1993.

This chapter has concentrated largely on questions of image, since these have helped the Conservatives to win four successive General Elections with a low and declining share of the vote: their particular assets had been the image of strong and decisive leadership, and competence and reliability in handling the economy. With the virtual disappearance of these assets the scene in the middle of 1993 offered very few signs of hope for the Conservatives, and it is remarkable how rapidly fortunes can change in a year or so. One crumb of comfort was that they had been in the same situation before and had come through to win: in addition, as discussed in the next chapter, there were few signs in by-elections of renewed confidence in Labour. Only in the next General Election shall we know how far the Conservatives have been prepared to go in policy and leadership to guarantee success, and whether they have been successful in prolonging their domination into the twenty-first century.

13
The Labour Party

Harold Wilson once described Labour as "the natural party of government". For the thirty years after the Second World War this looked to be a valid claim, at least in alternation with the Conservatives (Figure 13.1). In the thirty-four years from 1945 to 1979 the two major parties were in office for roughly half each. Up to 1970 Labour's share of the vote was never lower than 43%, they were ahead of the Conservatives in five of the eight General Elections, and were never more than 6% behind (Table 13.1). Thus the victory of 1964 was achieved with a share of the vote little greater than that in 1959 when they had lost by a hundred seats, confirming many of the assumptions about 'swing' discussed in Chapter 1.

The position was radically different after 1970: Labour never had more than 40% of the vote, even when in government, only

Table 13.1 *Conservative and Labour vote-share, 1945–1970*

	Con.	Lab.	Lab.lead
1945	39.8	48.3	+8.5
1950	43.5	46.1	+2.6
1951	48.0	48.8	+0.8
1955	49.7	46.4	−3.3
1959	49.4	43.8	−5.6
1964	43.4	44.1	+0.7
1966	41.9	47.9	+6.0
1970	46.4	43.0	−3.4

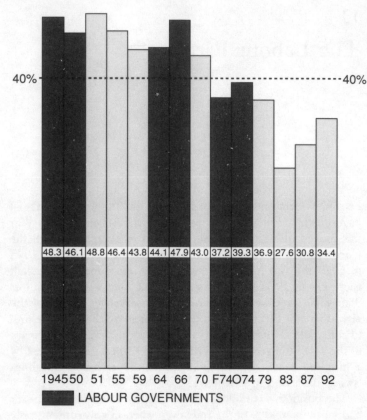

48.3 | 46.1 | 48.8 | 46.4 | 43.8 | 44.1 | 47.9 | 43.0 | 37.2 | 39.3 | 36.9 | 27.6 | 30.8 | 34.4

1945 50 51 55 59 64 66 70 F74 O74 79 83 87 92

■ LABOUR GOVERNMENTS

Fig. 13.1   Labour vote-share, 1945–1992

once did they have more than the Conservatives, and the margins were generally far greater (Table 13.2). Even in October 1974 they lost 190,000 votes in comparison with their result in February. Their results in 1983 and 1987 were their lowest since 1923, when they had fielded far fewer candidates. The same is true of numbers of votes. Apart from the unusual circumstances of 1945, when Labour's 48.3% consisted of 11.6 million, their vote fell below 12.2 million only in 1970, having reached a peak of nearly 14 million in 1951. Since 1970 the Labour vote was

Table 13.2 *Conservative and Labour vote-share, 1974–1992*

	Con.	Lab.	Lab. "lead"
Feb. 1974	37.8	37.2	−0.6
Oct. 1974	35.8	39.3	+3.5
1979	43.9	36.9	−7.0
1983	42.4	27.6	−14.8
1987	42.2	30.8	−11.4
1992	41.9	34.4	−6.5

never more than 11.7 million, and at its lowest in 1983 was under 8.5 million. Thus from a position where Labour seemed be firmly established, holding office for eleven of the fifteen years from 1964 to 1979, they had deteriorated to a point where many were asking "Can Labour ever win again?" and nearly as many were giving the answer 'No, not on their own' with varying degrees of force.

From the point of view of the election analyst, Labour's performance since 1970 raises two questions: how did they get to this position from an apparent position of strength in the 1960s and much of the 1970s; and what could they do to regain this dominance? The answer to the first question lies in a combination of class support and "identifiers" (Table 13.3). Labour's recovery among middle-class voters, though still only at the levels of 1966–1970, was not enough to compensate for

Table 13.3 *Support for Labour by social class, 1964–1992*

	AB	C1	C2	DE
1964	9	25	54	59
1966	15	30	58	65
1970	10	30	55	57
Feb. 1974	10	21	47	54
Oct. 1974	12	24	49	57
1979	22		42	49
1983	10	20	32	41
1987	14	21	36	48
1992	17	28	40	48

their serious losses among their traditional base in the working class. Since 1979 Labour had less than half the vote in the solid working class, and their share of the skilled working class was barely two-thirds of its 1966 level. In 1983 and 1987 Labour actually had less of the C2 vote than the Conservatives, something explained by the perceptions of the 'new' working class discussed in the previous chapter.

Table 13.4   *The "Old" Working class, 1983–1992*

	1983		1987		1992	
	Con.	Lab.	Con.	Lab.	Con.	Lab.
Lives in north	32	42	29	57	23	52
Council tenant	19	57	25	57	20	57
Public sector	29	46	32	49	36	48
Union member	(1992 only)				29	55

Labour was still strong among the "old" working class (Table 13.4), but unfortunately for Labour's chances all these areas showed a steady decline: for example at the time of the 1992 General Election only 30% of manual workers were council tenants against 57% who were owner-occupiers. Labour membership had also been falling: by the summer of 1992 it was down to a post-war low of about 253,000 compared with more than a million in the 1950s.

There was also a decline in the intensity of support for Labour. During the 1970s it was widely assumed that Labour supporters were as loyal as those of the Conservatives, and this reinforced the view that the Conservatives were condemned to a permanent second place. This was not the case: as the figures show, identification with Labour was in decline (Table 13.5). To make matters worse, Labour never succeeded in gaining the votes of all those who regarded themselves as Labour supporters even in winning years. Thus the proportion of voters regarding themselves as Labour supporters fell by over a quarter, and as strong Labour supporters by over a half. The gap between supporters and actual voters partly reflects Labour's problems at particular times: disappointment in 1970, disillusionment with

Table 13.5 *Labour identifiers, 1966–1992*

	Identifiers	Strong identifiers	Vote-share
1966	50	24	48
1970	47	21	43
1974 (average)	45	16	38
1979	42	11	37
1983	37	11	28
1987	36	13	31
1992	37	11	34

both major parties in 1974 and in 1983 deep distrust of the direction which Labour was taking, partly an underlying loss of confidence in politicians of all parties.

1983 marked the lowest point of Labour's post-war fortunes, and a clear rejection by the electorate of the left-wing policies which the party had adopted in the wake of the 1979 defeat. The period between 1983 and 1987 demonstrated a number of other problems for Labour whose solution seemed to be outside their control. The first was the geographical concentration of votes. Labour's support increased in those areas where they were already strong, and not in areas of Conservative strength. In the second quarter of 1989, for example, Labour had a lead of 5% nationally, but in the south-east the Conservatives still led by 17%, and 25% if London was excluded. It was calculated that this concentration meant that as long as the Conservatives could hold around 40% of the vote Labour would need 45%-46% for an overall majority rather than the 37%-38% which seemed to be their natural level.

Labour made considerable attempts before the 1987 General Election to resolve those difficulties which were soluble. They had changed their leaders, replacing Michael Foot and Denis Healey with the "dream ticket" of Neil Kinnock and Roy Hattersley, who in turn developed a range of policies which emphasised partnership with the unions and other interests, and increased spending on the welfare state in particular. The main threat to Labour's image, Militant and its involvement in local government was tackled with great determination and force, causing Kinnock's personal rating to soar, but also giving rise to the fear that he looked best when attacking his own side. Most significantly, Labour adopted many of the campaigning methods which had proved so successful for the Conservatives in 1983, and Kinnock's claim that Labour was a much better organisation with a better system for delivering its policies had a great deal of truth. Thus there was great disappointment in 1987 when the electorate showed that they still did not feel confident in Labour as a party of government, no matter how much they might like many of the policies put forward. Labour gained only 20 seats and an additional 3% of the vote compared with 1983. Their quantity and share of the vote were the second lowest post-war and their gains were made almost entirely at the expense of the Alliance.

The subsequent post-mortems suggested that the changes hitherto had been in presentation rather than substance, allowing the Conservatives to appear the party of radical change, so that a more fundamental review was needed. This took place over the next two years, and every Labour policy of the post-war period was considered and reshaped. Clause 4 of the party's constitution, committing it to public ownership "of the means of production, distribution and exchange" was effectively abandoned, with the admission that it would be neither possible nor desirable to re-nationalise the utilities privatised by the Conservatives now that so many had become share-owners. The days of high taxation were over, it was claimed, and necessary spending on welfare and the National Health Service would be met from growth in the economy: essentially Labour were saying that they would adopt many of the principles of the market economy, but would run it better than the Conservatives, a position little different from the old SDP. Defence had been a deeply divisive issue for Labour since the 1950s, but unilateral disarmament had only become official party policy after 1979. The policy had been repudiated by senior Labour figures, and had clearly helped to lose the 1983 election. In 1987 the time-scale had been changed, but the commitment had not: nuclear weapons would be removed within the lifetime of a parliament rather than "from day one". The break-up of the old Soviet bloc on the one hand and the Gulf War on the other enabled Labour to advocate reduction instead of abandonment, while at the same time arguing that the "peace dividend" would help their programmes of public spending.

Perhaps the most remarkable feature of Labour's policy review was the way in which it was accepted by the party. In theory the leader is expected to respond to the membership, rather than the other way round, and Labour leaders in opposition, particularly Hugh Gaitskell, had found great difficulty in carrying through radical initiatives. In spite of the complaints of Tony Benn and others that Labour was no longer a party of debate, the proposals in the policy review were approved by the Party Conferences with little trouble, showing that Neil Kinnock had a degree of domination over the party almost unknown even when Labour was in government, let alone in opposition after losing three General Elections.

That was the priority, of course: to win the next election, not just for the sake of being in office, but also to put right what was perceived as the harm done during the Thatcher years. Once again the strategy failed, and Labour lost in 1992. The reasons for loss are inevitably bound up with what should be done to try and win next time. If Labour can win on their own, as they did in the 1960s and 1970s, then all they have to do is to eliminate those defects which cost them victory in 1992: if not, then they will have to find some more radical approach to the challenge of forming a government.

The first scenario is often termed "one last heave". It is based on the assumption that Labour nearly won, and can bring it off with a little more effort. The main evidence for this rests in Labour's recovery from the trough of 1983, and particularly since 1987. They gained 42 seats, more than twice their increase 1983–1987, and though their share of the vote was still their third lowest post-war, their quantity of votes, at 11.56 million, was their best since February 1974, more than they had had in October 1974, when they had achieved an overall majority and over 1.5 million more than in 1987. As discussed in Chapter 1, the electoral system seemed at last to be working in Labour's favour. A further 1.5 million votes would bring them close to the levels of 1966, and a further 42 seats would bring them within striking distance of a majority, and almost certainly make them the largest party in a hung parliament.

There was further encouragement from looking at Labour's support in class terms in 1992. They had certainly made significant progress among AB and C1 voters, with one survey giving them 17% of AB and 28% of C1, another 23% and 29% respectively, certainly their best figures for "middle-class" voters since 1966. The findings on C2 voters are less clear, though Labour seem to have reached 40% again for the first time since 1979, but one survey has this 5% ahead of the Conservatives, another 1% behind. Their share of DE voters was anything between 48% and 57%, 19–23% ahead of the Conservatives, depending upon which survey you believe. The problems for the government after 1992, and the slump in the electorate's confidence must have made many Labour supporters believe that they had only to sit tight and avoid making mistakes to win.

The Labour leadership did not fall into this trap, but many believed that if Labour could resolve the remaining problems of their internal structure and relationships they would be much better placed to win. Neil Kinnock had attempted to reduce the power of trade unions in the selection of parliamentary candidates and the election of the leader by replacing their "block vote" by "one member, one vote", and after the 1992 defeat the new leader, John Smith, saw this as vital to Labour's future success. This policy proved divisive within the party, with some arguing the need for Labour to reduce its links with unions in order to appeal to new voters, rather as Gaitskell had tried in the 1950s, and others that the party could not afford to cut itself off from its historical and financial roots. These divisions were apparent among trade union leaders as well. Bill Jordan, leader of the Engineering and Electricians, argued that failure to accept the proposals could cost Labour future victory, but it became clear by the summer of 1993 that enough of the biggest unions could oppose the changes to defeat them at the Party Conference. Even John Smith's concession that unions should still be involved in leadership elections was not enough to prevent the two biggest unions from confirming their opposition. Thus the controversies concerning union involvement in Labour policy (as when the TGWU voted against the abandonment of unilateralism in 1988) and in the mandatory reselection of candidates, with such episodes as alleged infiltration by Militant in Birkenhead at the beginning of 1990 seemed unlikely to be resolved: the whole question of union links seemed to confirm Tony Blair's complaint in a television discussion a year after the 1992 defeat that Labour seemed to have the capacity to undermine itself.

In the same discussion Roy Hattersley argued that Labour has only succeeded when it has had "a big idea". In 1945 this was a programme of welfare and public ownership designed to take advantage of the mood for change after the Second World War: in 1964 the image of progress compared with the old-fashioned Tories. In Hattersley's view Labour had been too concerned in 1987 and 1992 to emphasise what they were not: to reassure voters that a Labour government would not be harmful rather than projecting it as a new opportunity. One such idea has been constitutional reform. Labour had attempted modest reforms of the House of Lords between 1966 and 1968, but otherwise did not propose significant changes until the late 1980s under the influence of such initiatives as "Charter 88". One of the most significant changes considered was reform of the voting system as Labour figures from both right and left of the party argued that they could not win again under "first past the post". The general possibilities and implications are considered in the final chapter, but as with the issue of internal democracy, voting reform has shown many of Labour's current problems. A commission was set up under Professor Raymond (now Lord) Plant of Southampton University which finally reported in 1993. The interim report seemed to favour the Additional Member System as used in Germany, but the final report recommended something much more cautious, the Supplementary Vote,

"It's just a PR exercise"

†Private Eye

whereby voters would be able to express first and second
preferences, which would apply only to elections for a new
second chamber, replacing the House of Lords, and possibly the
European Parliament, but not the House of Commons.

Many of the supporters of voting reform within the Labour
Party were the same people who favoured reducing the links with
the unions, seeing both as part of the process of modernising the
party, but many who favoured other reforms objected to changing the voting system. Some, such as Roy Hattersley, felt that it
would be tantamount to conceding that Labour could not win
again, and would guarantee that third parties would hold the
balance of power: after a General Election Labour would need
to go to the Liberals and say "which of our election promises do
you want us to break?" Others, such as Labour's "First Past the
Post Group", set up in May 1993 to combat the Plant Report,
complained that once again Labour was wasting time on unimportant questions instead of attacking the government and
establishing their own individual political identity. John Smith

attempted to avoid a serious split by agreeing that there should be a referendum on voting reform when Labour regains power: but if they do come to office under the present system there will be no need to change it.

The question "Can Labour win again?" has aroused strong passions among politicians and analysts: clearly a definite answer is only possible with each General Election. On the one hand Labour have lost four times in a row in spite of their best efforts, and most of the underlying trends seem to be against them. On the other hand the result in 1992 had some encouraging features, and during the following months the Conservatives became increasingly unpopular, reaching new lows throughout the first half of 1993. Opinion polls showed Labour still below 50%, and largely static on general support and leadership. In the Newbury by-election the Labour candidate lost his deposit, suggesting, as one analyst put it, that voters who opposed the Conservatives were prepared to vote for any party provided it was not Labour. The Labour Party will certainly fight the next General Election on their own, but unless they win decisively they will probably not survive long into the twenty-first century.

14
Third parties

It is unfortunate, but unavoidable, that the term "Third parties" should be applied to those parties which put up candidates consistently at elections, campaign on all the major issues rather than one or two, cover the whole country rather than being confined to one region, as is the case with the nationalist parties, but which stand no chance of forming a government except as a junior partner to one of the parties of government. Until the end of the nineteenth century there was no national third party, the nearest being the large number of Irish MPs campaigning for Home Rule, but from 1900 there was a unified Labour Group, the Labour Representation Committee. After the First World War and the split in the Liberal Party Labour grew in importance until they were in a position to overtake the Liberals as the main alternative to the Conservatives, forming governments with Liberal support in 1924 and 1929.

After the Second World War it seemed as though the Liberals were on the point of disappearing, but they survived to maintain a significant third-party presence on the political scene. Until 1981 they were on their own, but the creation of the Social Democratic Party added another third party, in many ways complementary. The uneasy alliance between the two did not survive the 1987 General Election, but after the merger and its difficulties the Liberals re-emerged apparently little weaker.

The fortunes of third parties since the war show their strengths and weaknesses (Figure 14.1). The ability to retain

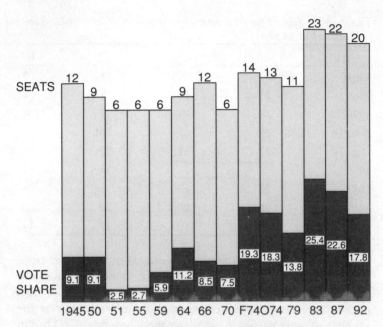

Fig. 14.1   Liberal support, 1945–1992

seats even when voting support slumps, as in 1950 and 1951, shows the importance of concentration in a particular area, just as the elections of 1983 and 1987 worked against the Alliance and in favour of Labour for the same reason. Later elections emphasise the problem already outlined in earlier chapters: that third party support is very even rather than having a secure base in any one class or interest, as the class support for the Liberals and Alliance since 1964 shows (Table 14.1). These figures also show the way in which the rise and fall of support is even across the classes, and the same would be true of analysis by age or gender.

One major reason for this is that support for third parties has mainly been based on protest rather than policies, in other words voters are showing what they do not like about the party for which they have previously voted, and probably a lack of

Table 14.1 *Support for third parties by social class, 1964–1992. (figures to nearest whole number)*

	AB	C1	C2	DE
1964	15	14	11	9
1966	11	11	8	7
1970	10	9	7	6
Feb. 74	20	25	20	19
Oct. 74	22	21	20	16
1979	16		15	13
1983	28	27	26	24
1987	26	26	22	20
1992	20	19	17	14

confidence in the major alternative, rather than anything positive about third parties. Protest voting is much more common in by-elections, and as party allegiances have become weaker, so third parties have seen an increasing number of successes at the expense of other parties, particularly the Conservatives. Thus in 1962 the Liberals were able to capitalise on the Tories' fading image in winning Orpington; between 1970 and 1974 they took such safe seats as Ely and Ripon. In the by-elections between 1983 and 1987 the Alliance averaged 40% of the vote compared with about 30% for each of the major parties. The Conservatives lost support in all fourteen of the by-elections of the period, and Labour in ten, while the Alliance lost support in only two. The break-up of the Alliance in 1987–1988 distorts any direct comparison for the period 1987–1992, but by comparison with the General Election of 1987 support rose by nearly 19% at Epping Forest (December 1988) and over 27% at Richmond in the following February, though in neither case was this enough to wrest the seat from the Conservatives. Once Liberal support began to recover they did take seats: in the Eastbourne by-election their support rose by 21%, at Ribble Valley by 27% and even in Kincardine and Deeside by 13%. Even though by-elections are by their nature unpredictable, it is clear that these increases represented great disquiet among voters at some of the things which the government was doing, even if, as in Ribble Valley, it was to a great extent annoyance at a popular MP (David Waddington) being moved to the House of Lords.

The fate of all these seats in the 1992 General Election highlights another problem for third parties: maintaining the momentum into a General Election. Throughout the post-war period, with the exception of 1987–1992, assumptions have been made based on by-elections which have proved to be unfounded in practice. In February 1974 the Liberals lost most of the seats they had gained since 1970, even though their share of the vote increased during the campaign from 12% at the outset to over 19% on polling day. At their peak the SDP had 29 MPs: in the 1983 General Election they lost all but 6. In 1992 the Conservatives regained every seat lost in by-elections since 1987. The problem is not just one of protest: in a by-election parties can deploy all their resources both financial and personal, and it is much more difficult when fighting hundreds of seats, especially since 1983, the first time that a third party grouping put candidates into every seat outside Northern Ireland. In that year there was apparently only £80 available to the two SDP candidates in Coventry. Key party figures cannot afford to jeopardise their own seats to carry out a major national campaign, and it is rare for this to work in a party's favour, as it did for Jeremy Thorpe in February 1974.

The evidence suggests that many third-party voters stay for only one election, and having changed once are readier to change again. Some voters feel that protest is less appropriate in a General Election, when a government is being chosen rather than just one MP: this point was made repeatedly at Eastbourne and Monmouth, with voters saying that they usually voted Conservative, and would do so again once they had made their point. In addition the major parties have been at pains to emphasise, particularly in 1987 and 1992, that a vote for third parties could let in the party the voter most dislikes: for example in 1987 68% of a survey believed that a vote for the Alliance would at best be wasted and at worst positively harmful.

Third parties are usually dependent on the other parties to provide the opportunities to establish a clear identity. The more usual scenario is that the Conservative and Labour Parties are extreme right or left, and therefore third parties can occupy the middle ground. This was the argument in the 1950s and 1960s, and revived after the 1979 General Election, with Mrs Thatcher in charge of the Conservatives and Labour dominated by its left wing, receiving its most developed analysis in Roy Jenkins's Dimbleby Lecture in November 1979, which provided the theoretical basis for the formation of the SDP. In their 1987 manifesto the Alliance argued that "For many the situation seems hopeless. Unable to contemplate five more years of uncaring government under Mrs Thatcher, they still do not trust the Labour Party. Mr Kinnock tries hard, but how long can he keep the lid on the extremists of the Left? . . . We would curb the Tories' divisive policies and stop the destructive antics of the Labour Left". By 1992, however, the situation was much more like that in the 1970s, when the two parties of government were seen as broadly similar in their policies and in their inability to solve the problems. With Labour adopting most of the policies usually termed "social democrat" and the Conservatives moving away from many of the more doctrinaire aspects of Thatcherism, the middle ground was now occupied, which meant that the Liberals' 1992 manifesto had little to say about the other parties, asserting that "this manifesto offers a different choice for Britain." Such a position reinforces their identity as a party of protest.

Even if third parties succeed in making alternative policies attractive, they are dependent upon the major parties to put them into effect. This is the classic dilemma for all third parties: independence or power? In 1974 there were soundings between the Liberal and Conservative leadership, but the Liberals were not clear what they wanted, and by October had realised that their claims to be different would be compromised by too close an association with either Tories or Labour, and could cost them votes. It was claimed that the Lib.-Lab. pact of the later 1970s would represent a restraining influence on a rampantly socialist government, but this is not really justified in view of the personality of the Prime Minister James Callaghan and the other external restraints on the government's actions. Opponents of the pact were probably right when they blamed the pact for the decline in the Liberal vote in 1979.

The Alliance between the Liberals and the Social Democratic Party from 1981 to 1987 did not bring about any fundamental change in the position and problems of third parties. Certainly for the first year or so it looked as though the claim to be "breaking the mould" might be justified as SDP leaders and Alliance candidates won seats which had been safe for the Conservatives for many years, and people joined the SDP who had never previously belonged to any political party. They had leaders with experience of Cabinet office at the highest level, but were determined not to be leader-dominated: policy was to be made, and candidates selected by the membership as a whole, through conferences and postal ballots. But the problems began very early. The Falklands War showed how easily issues can change, and the difficulty of providing a plausible alternative when public opinion strongly supports the government. Local elections in May 1982 saw the SDP win barely 20% of the seats won by the Liberals, and the 1983 General Election confirmed the difficulty of turning votes into seats.

Table 14.2 *Increases in third party support*

	AB	C1	C2	DE	Overall
1970–1974	10	16	13	10	12
1979–1983	12	12	11	11	11

The 1983 result showed that the SDP in fact made very little difference to third party fortunes. Certainly the Alliance vote was greater than anything achieved by the Liberals post-war, but there were many more candidates than when they scored their previous highest, February 1974. In class terms, the improvements 1970–1974 and 1979–1983 were very similar, as Table 14.2 shows. The SDP did not secure enough votes to retain more than 5 of the seats they held going into the election, and their support made little difference in the seats which the Liberals hoped to win.

The change of leader after 1983 made little difference to the overall pattern of by-election successes and General Election disappointment, as Labour regained some of the lost ground: in 1987 the Alliance lost 2% among AB voters, 1% in C1 and 4% in C2 and DE compared with 1983. The seats which were safe for the Alliance in 1987 were those where the Liberals were already strong, not where Labour dominated. This was confirmed by regional analysis. Between 1983 and 1987 the Alliance lost 2.5% overall: their lowest loss (0.1%) was in the south-east outside London and the south-west, where Labour did worst; their highest in the north of England (4%) and Scotland and Wales (5%) where Labour did best. The Alliance also showed the difficulties of co-operation for two distinct parties with strong personalities as leader and with differing policies on key issues such as defence and education. Even organisation caused problems, with the SDP strong in London and the Liberals at their strongest in the regions: in 1987 each party had a separate budget, and was not prepared to make money available to pay for centrally-funded advertising.

The break-up of the Alliance and the collapse of the SDP after the 1987 election has already been discussed in Chapter 11, and the main question here is whether the Liberals could survive. For a long time it looked as though they had been seriously damaged. Findings from the Gallup 9000 chart their decline: from 23.1% in the General Election their support fell to 18.4% after the merger, 12.1% after the Owen breakaway, 10.1% at the time of Ashdown's election in August 1988 and 8.8% in May 1989, with Ashdown's personal rating about the same. In the elections to the European parliament in June 1989 they scored 6%, and were nearly bankrupt. A year later they had clambered back to 9.3%, but had made little impact otherwise: 72% were unsure of the party's name, only 2% knew what they stood for, and only 8% had strong views about the Liberals.

Soon after this, in October 1990, the Liberals scored one of those spectacular successes which are now much more likely,

winning Eastbourne and nearly doubling their vote. Leaving
aside local factors such as an unwise choice of candidate by the
Conservatives, and some extremely unwise remarks that a vote
against the Conservatives was a vote for the IRA (the by-election
had been caused by the murder of Ian Gow, a noted supporter
of the unionist cause who had resigned over the Anglo-Irish
Agreement in 1985), this was a major coup for the Liberals,
and a sign that they had to be taken seriously again. Their
subsequent fortunes in by-elections varied (Table 14.3), but they
saw their support increase in 6 of the remaining 10, and won 2
more seats, in spite of some complaints that the Liberals had
little specific to offer.

Table 14.3 *Liberal results in by-elections, October 1990–November 1991*

	1987 General Election	By-election	Change
Eastbourne*	29.7	50.8	+21.2
Bootle	13.0	7.8	−5.2
Bradford North	17.7	25.2	+7.5
Paisley North	15.8	8.3	−7.5
Paisley South	15.1	9.8	−5.3
Ribble Valley*	21.4	48.5	+27.1
Monmouth	24.0	24.8	+0.8
Liverpool Walton	21.2	36.0	+14.8
Kincardine*	36.3	49.0	+12.7
Hemsworth	15.8	20.1	+4.3
Langbaurgh	19.9	16.1	−3.8

(* denotes seats won)

In one sense the 1992 General Election was disappointing,
since they lost every seat they had won in by-elections and lost
three more, two to Conservatives, one to Plaid Cymru, though
they won four seats, including unseating Chris Patten at Bath,
giving them 20 in all. They saw their share of the vote fall to
17.8%, a loss of nearly 5% compared with 1987. Yet the
Liberals would also be justified in feeling a certain amount of
satisfaction. They had matched the target they had set themselves at their lowest, that they would hold 20 seats: and they
had kept a large part of the vote which the SDP had brought

with them, in net terms. Only in 1974, 1983 and 1987 had they achieved a higher share of the vote, and they had secured nearly 6 million votes, their fourth highest number of votes post-war: this compared with 7.8 million in 1983 and 7.3 million in 1987. As Figure 14.1 showed earlier in this chapter, the "underlying trend" has been upwards for the Liberals since 1970, with the low points getting higher as well as the peaks, and the Liberals gaining at least 13% of the vote and 4 million votes in each of the last six General Elections.

The Liberals' position as the main party of protest was confirmed with the first by-election of the 1992 parliament, in May 1993 as a result of the sudden death of Judith Chaplin, the MP for Newbury and one of John Major's closest friends and advisers. The Liberals had come second in 1992, and though they had trailed by over 12,000, they were hopeful that they could take the seat. The result must have exceeded their wildest dreams. The Conservatives lost 29% of their General Election vote, far more than anything between 1987 and 1992, and the Liberals had a majority of more than 22,000. The swing, 28.4%, was the biggest since Sutton and Cheam and the Isle of Ely in 1972. Taken in conjunction with the same day's county council results it confirmed the poll findings discussed in Chapter 12 that the government had become the most unpopular since the war, and supported the conventional wisdom that discontented Tories vote Liberal, especially in by-elections, whatever happens in General Elections.

The Liberals' lowest point after 1987 coincided with the high point for the other significant third party of the late 1980s, the Green Party. As the Ecology Party they had been putting up candidates since February 1974, though they did not average more than 2% in the constituencies they fought, and were only able to field 106 candidates in 1983 and 133 in 1987. In the 1989 European elections they gained 14.9%, which would have been enough under a proportional system to give them 15 seats, though under our system they did not gain any. With the Liberals on 6.2% in the same elections in spite of their "European" credentials, it looked briefly as though the Greens might represent a significant challenger for the position of main third party.

The fate of the Greens since then provides a microcosm of the problems of third parties. In the first place they were seen as a single-issue party, without the ability to put their programme into practice. Thus they were powerless to prevent the hijacking of environmental policies by the other parties, most notably by Mrs Thatcher in a speech to the Royal Society in September 1988, when she claimed that the Conservatives were now the most truly Green Party. At their Annual Conference in 1989 they turned their back on any anti-Conservative pact, and decided against appointing a figure-head leader, crucial in these days of "presidential" leaders and "sound-bites". Their best-known figure, former footballer and sports commentator David Icke, did a great deal of harm to the Green cause in 1991 when he claimed to be the Son of God and that the world would end in 1997, and a thunderous denunciation by Jonathon Porritt did little to repair the damage. In the 1992 General Election the Greens fielded 253 candidates, but their fate was the same as in previous elections: apart from 3.8% in Islington North their candidates mainly scored 1–2%: from 2 million votes in 1989 they fell to 171,000 as voters made up their minds on economic rather than environmental issues.

Things got worse in the months following the general election when the Greens' leading figure Sara Parkin decided to quit, and in her resignation letter said that she could "see no point in squandering my time, energy and spirit on fighting endless redundant skirmishes behind the barricades ... I have been forced to the conclusion that the Green Party has become a liability to green politics." Jonathon Porritt made the same point a few days later, describing the Green Party as "squandering talent and commitment more profligately than Brazil squanders its rainforests" and as "an inward-looking, permanently divided organisation" which was rendering itself all but invisible and opting for "self-indulgent fundamentalism" in the same way as other Green Parties in Europe. His article ended "The future of Green politics in the UK is very much up for grabs. Yet it would seem that the Green party itself hasn't a clue how to make a fist of it." With this condemnation from a former chairman there would seem to be little hope for the Green party as at present constituted.

All this leaves the Liberals as the only significant third party within the definition at the start of this chapter, as they have been since the Second World War. During that time the question "is Britain a two-party system?" has had a variety of answers, coming closest to being true in the 1950s. Under our present electoral system two parties are likely to dominate in the House of Commons, and on issues it has always proved difficult for third parties to establish a distinctive point of view. Looking at shares of the vote gives a different answer, especially since 1970 (Figure 14.2). Whereas in the 1950s third parties were totalling less than 4% of the vote, since 1970 they have gained

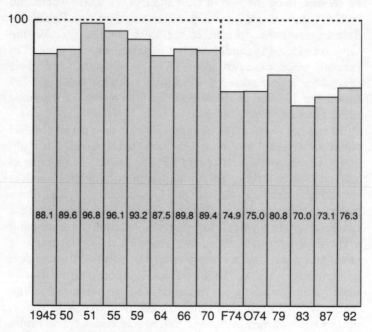

Fig. 14.2   "Two-party" vote, 1945–1992

20–30% as voters move away from strong alignment with the traditional parties. Clearly there are plenty of votes available for third parties, but without electoral reform winning seats will continue to depend on by-elections and the performance of the other parties.

15
Nationalist parties

With the obvious exception of Ireland, the United Kingdom has not been greatly affected by nationalism in the twentieth century. There have been sporadic attempts to create English nationalist parties, such as Richard Acland's Commonwealth Party after the war and the various incarnations of the National Front discussed below: more recently developments in the European Community have enabled a strongly nationalist strain to develop within the Conservative Party, though there is no sign of any separation. Scottish and Welsh nationalism can also be found in the Labour Party, but in their case separate nationalist parties emerged and survived: there has been at least one nationalist Member of Parliament since 1966.

All the nationalist parties have seen their fortunes rise and fall since they first became significant in the late 1960s and 1970s. The main reason for this is that like the other 'third parties' in the British system their support is almost entirely based on protest, and so fluctuates according to issues. For the National Front these issues are social and economic: Plaid Cymru combines and supports similar issues with cultural nostalgia: the Scottish National Party is the most overtly political with its insistence on revising or even destroying the relationship between Scotland and the rest of the United Kingdom. The implications of such changes are considered in the final chapter: in this chapter the emphasis will be on the impact of nationalist parties on post-war elections and the reasons for their support.

The National Front and the British National Party

Though the National Front was formed in 1967 when three smaller right-wing organisations merged, it achieved little impact for several years. Its peak of influence came in the mid-1970s: in 1974 its 90 candidates averaged nearly 3% of the vote. Their main basis of support was the growing fear among working class voters in big cities that increasing immigration would threaten jobs, and possibly a whole way of life. There was also a feeling among some middle class voters that the Labour government was powerless to prevent a steady shift to the left, and that only a strong right-wing party could achieve a reversal: at least one of the National Front's parliamentary candidates in 1979 was explicitly fighting a perceived left-wing domination in education. This view in a less extreme form led to the formation of such pressure groups as the Freedom Association.

The most noticeable result of the growth in support for the National Front was in the field of Direct Action, especially a series of marches in major cities which provoked a reaction from the left, mainly in the form of the Anti-Nazi League. There were frequent clashes between the two sets of supporters and problems for the police in holding them apart or regulating the holding of marches. In addition to this increased prominence, the National Front was achieving good results in by-elections even in constituencies where there were very few immigrants.

This encouraged the National Front to field over 300 candidates in the 1979 General Election, though many of them did not trouble to visit their constituencies, and to try to develop a range of policies based on economic nationalism such as central direction of the economy and attacks on the European Community. This was unsuccessful to the point of humiliation. In interviews they proved incapable of explaining their policies, and on polling day they gained around a thousand votes in inner cities such as London or Leicester, a few hundred elsewhere, averaging barely six hundred votes per candidate.

As a result the National Front saw a sharp decline in its fortunes. In the first place there was a split, with John Tyndall setting up the British National Party, which has since become the principal voice of the fascist right. The General Election had confirmed that voters are reluctant to protest when a government is at stake, especially in an election as important as that of 1979. In addition, statements by Mrs Thatcher and others had suggested that some of the concerns of those who had voted for the National Front before 1979 would be addressed: this was confirmed when the Conservatives introduced the Commonwealth Immigrants Act, which became law in 1981, imposing further restrictions on immigration.

The parties of the fascist right took little part in the General Election of 1983 and opted out altogether in 1987, blaming the increase in the deposit to £500. Since then there has been something of a revival, for which some of the reasons are domestic, some international. At home, some of the far right have exploited heavy metal and skin-head bands, as well as their more traditional area of football support, which may have an influence on young male voters. On the international scene, the Front National in France achieved its support for much the same reasons as its counterpart in Britain, the loss of jobs in areas of high immigration such as Marseilles. Events in Eastern Europe after 1989 created a similar situation in Germany, where there has been a resurgence of far right activity: the most serious example was the fire-bombing of an immigrant hostel, but there have been numerous demonstrations as workers from the former West Germany come to terms with the implications of an influx of workers from the East and the strains of coupling two disparate economies. There have been right-wing, racist groups develop in countries as diverse as Austria, where Jorg Haider has openly praised "the correct employment policies of Nazi Germany", Poland, Spain and Hungary.

Though there is little direct connection with Britain, the British National Party has profited from the added prominence of the far right in Europe. They now have 43 branches and had 12 candidates in the 1992 General Election, though this is far short of their showing in 1970, and their average vote was only just over 500: the National Front's 14 candidates averaged only just over 300.

It is unlikely that the BNP will have a significant electoral future in Britain, on the evidence of the past. There is no sign of a revival comparable with that of the 1970s, and the only substantial nationalist issue in British politics in the 1990s concerns the European Community and its development towards a more federal system. Opposition to these trends will come mainly from Conservative "Euro-sceptics", who are the only people able to put pressure on the government. As usual in these circumstances, there is no place for smaller parties once a major party takes on an issue.

Plaid Cymru

Although Plaid Cymru was the first of the nationalist parties to achieve electoral success with the by-election victory in Carmarthen in 1966, their support in Wales has been small and their fortunes wavering in both seats and votes (Figure 15.1). Welsh nationalism first came on to the general political agenda in 1973 with the publication of the Kilbrandon Report, and this was made a practical necessity by the results in 1974 when the Labour government needed all the support they could get in the House of Commons in order to hang on to power. As already described in Chapter 8, devolution was decisively rejected in Wales in the referendum on 1 March 1979, and this was reflected in the General Election result, with a drop of over a quarter in their share of the vote and a loss of one seat. The next two General Elections showed a further decline in vote share, but no further loss in seats. The results indeed defied logic in that between 1983 and 1987 the vote share fell but Plaid Cymru gained an extra seat. In 1992 along with a marked increase in their vote they gained a fourth seat, supplanting the Scottish National Party as the largest nationalist party in the House of Commons. Whereas in 1987 Labour took votes from all three other parties, in 1992 Labour continued to rise, gaining almost half the votes in Wales (and 27 of the 38 seats) and it was the Conservatives and the Liberals who lost both votes and seats.

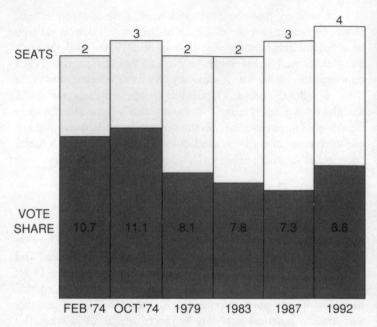

Fig. 15.1   Plaid Cymru: votes and seats

   This suggests that there has been a change in the nature of
support for Plaid Cymru. During the 1980s the main reasons
for voting Plaid Cymru seemed to be nostalgia for the Welsh
language and culture, which implied a continued decline as
voters died, and the party failed to broaden its support. With
little likelihood of any revival of Welsh devolution, opposed by
Mrs Thatcher and Neil Kinnock, Welsh nationalism seemed
fated to be confined to a handful of constituencies in the rural
west. More recently, however, there has been a growing
sense of a threat to jobs as well as to the culture as the
English population has grown to around half a million. By
the spring of 1993 mid- and north Wales had 20% of
'foreign' owner-occupiers: only inner London could show a
higher figure. In these regions the English are more likely be
employed in high-status jobs in the service sector, with a typical

situation being a shop with an English manager and Welsh sales staff.

The government would point to a number of measures designed to assist Wales: higher expenditure, the establishment of a Welsh Channel 4, a Welsh Language Bill which would place the two languages on an equal footing, and a reorganisation of Welsh local government into 21 unitary authorities (replacing the eight large counties of the 1974 system) to give the Welsh greater responsibility for their own affairs by 1995. The Plaid Cymru MPs generally get on well with the Welsh Office, since their main aim is to get the best deal they can for Wales, something likely to be enhanced by the development of the European Community Commission for the Regions.

This is unlikely to be enough to satisfy the demands usually associated with Meibion Glyndwr (the Sons of Glendower). The name first appeared in 1981, and since then there have been over 200 fire-bombings of Welsh holiday cottages in English ownership, English settlers and estate agents dealing in Welsh property sales to the English as far afield as London. This took a nasty turn in the spring of 1993, when thirteen English families received an ultimatum to leave Wales by St David's Day (1 March). Though apparently nothing happened, two families decided to quit, and others were refused insurance cover. This would be serious enough if it were just confined to a handful of extremists, but polls indicate that a majority sympathises with Meibion Glyndwr aims though they deprecate their methods. Young people particularly resent the English penetration in jobs, and in a Channel 4 programme many said that new English settlers would face broken windows and graffiti at least. If these young people turn to Plaid Cymru as a means of expressing their discontent there could be a further increase in support which could threaten the few remaining Conservative seats and even some of those held by Labour. The government clearly feels that it has gone far enough in satisfying Welsh needs, and Labour's manifesto contained only a commitment to an elected Welsh assembly "in the lifetime of a full parliament" in addition to the most recent Conservative policies. The important question is

whether the new generation of discontented Welsh will regard
Plaid Cymru as the means of achieving their aims, or irrelevant.
Certainly it would be unwise for current analysts to dismiss Plaid
Cymru, as *The British General Election of 1966* did as "a useful
refuge for older Liberals and young romantic idealists."

The Scottish National Party

The fortunes of the Scottish National Party have seen similar
ups and downs to those of Plaid Cymru though more extreme
(Figure 15.2). Their rise in the 1970s was meteoric, and their
fall after the collapse of the possiblity of devolution equally swift.
Their decline continued in 1983, down to a level little above that
of 1970, but 1987 saw a significant revival, continued in 1992,
though this was not reflected in seats: indeed the SNP emerged
from the 1992 General Election with fewer seats than Plaid
Cymru, in spite of hugely greater support.

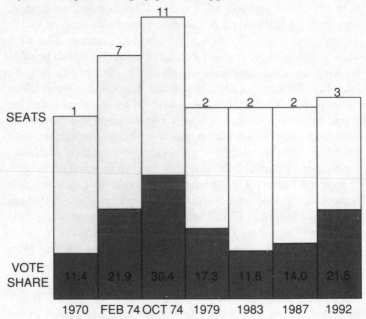

Fig. 15.2   Scottish National Party: votes and seats.

The revival in 1987 seemed particularly significant because it coincided with a slump in Tory fortunes to their lowest level in seats and votes (Figure 15.3). The SNP looked to have recovered from the problems of the earlier 1980s when they lost a number of key figures. But the SNP optimism overlooked the fact that Labour had gained more (up 7.3.%) from the collapse of the Conservatives and the Alliance (down by 4.4% and 5.3% respectively) compared with 1983 than had the SNP (up 2.2%) and that they were still below their 1979 figure. Such considerations seemed irrelevant when Jim Sillars won the Govan by-election in November 1988. The SNP had come fourth in 1987, but Labour's majority of 19509 was replaced by an SNP majority of 3,554, a swing of 28%: the Conservative vote was halved, and the Liberal Democrat lost two-thirds of the earlier Alliance vote. At their next Annual Conference, in September 1989 SNP leaders claimed around 28% of the Scottish vote, a figure in line with earlier opinion polls: this gave the confidence to launch their new policy of independence within Europe, reversing their opposition to Europe in the 1970s. By the beginning of 1990 there had been a decline to less than 20%, and in the only other Scottish by-election of the 1987–1992 Parliament (Kincardine and Deeside) they scored 11%, though this nearly doubled their 1987 showing.

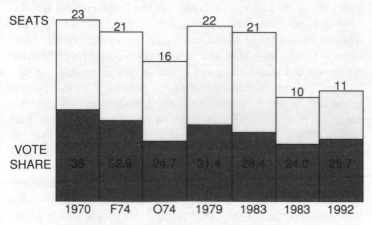

Fig. 15.3 Conservative support in Scotland

2   FRIDAY, APRIL 10, 1992

Poll predicts Tories cut to 3 in Scotland

©The Daily Telegraph

Opinion polls before the 1992 election were suggesting a further collapse in the Conservative vote, and a drop to four seats or less. The SNP were naturally expecting to benefit. In the event the Conservatives did significantly better, as already described. So, in votes, did the SNP: their 21.5% was their best result since October 1974, and only just below the level of February 1974. The rise in support of the Conservatives and the SNP at Labour's expense was further confirmed by a poll in the *Glasgow Herald* three weeks after polling day, and by the local election results on 9 May. But in terms of seats they were bitterly disappointed, losing Govan and retaining only three seats overall.

The 1992 result confirms all of the Scottish National Party's major difficulties. Unlike Plaid Cymru, with its closely concentrated support, the SNP now takes its vote from all areas and all classes. They had the largest share of the vote in one of Scotland's nine regions (Tayside, where they won one seat) and were second in two others (Grampian, where they won their two other seats, and Dumfries and Galloway). Another difficulty inherent in the current voting system is that it significantly discriminates against the SNP (Figure 15.4). They have never had more than half the seats that a proportional system would

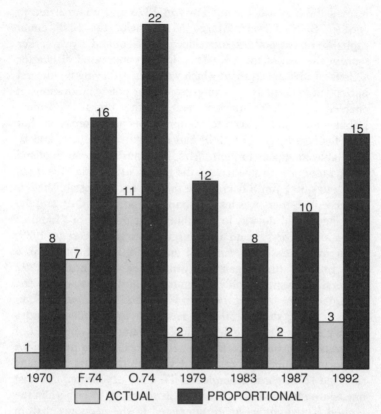

Fig. 15.4 Scottish National Party seats: actual and proportional

give, and usually the ratio has been nearer four or five to one between 'proportional' and actual seats.

There are three principal problems for the Scottish National Party apart from the structural ones, and all are inevitable for third parties in a fundamentally two-party system. The first is that much of their support is based on protest, and thus they are only likely to be successful when there is a combination of a convenient by-election and a major issue. This is what happened in Govan. As well as a strong candidate, Jim Sillars, who had formed the Scottish Labour Party in 1976 and was married to another SNP stalwart, Margo MacDonald, the SNP could capitalise on the poll tax, introduced into Scotland a year earlier than in the rest of the UK. This not only increased dislike for a Conservative government which was seen as having no interest in Scotland except as a proving-ground for policy innovations, it enabled the SNP to attack Labour. As the official opposition, Labour could not be seen to encourage people to break the law by refusing to pay. The SNP had no such inhibitions, and so were able to appear to fight "Mrs Thatcher's grip on Scotland much more effectively than . . . the feeble 50 Labour MPs up to now", to quote Jim Sillars. Once the poll tax was established, if not accepted, there was less reason to support the SNP, and the best they could do was to grumble about the use of "Land of Hope and Glory" in an Edinburgh Festival concert in 1989. Their main new issue, summed up as "A Free Scotland in a Free Europe" (the slogan with which they went into the 1992 General Election) was only intermittently attractive to the voters. Admittedly one opinion poll for ITN and "*The Scotsman*", in January 1992, showed 50% in favour of independence and a further 27% supporting devolution, as against 19% in favour of the *status quo*, but after the General Election the proportions supporting independence and devolution had almost exactly reversed (27% for independence, 47% for devolution). At least one analyst has asserted that Scottish voters, as elsewhere in the United Kingdom, are more interested in the economy than in constitutional relationships, and there Scotland has fared rather well. The Scottish economy is growing fast, Scotland has been less affected by the recession than elsewhere, in spite of such major closures as Ravenscraig, and spending per capita was nearly 24% higher in Scotland than in England in the year 1990–1991. In this respect, at least, the SNP would appear to need a new big issue.

The question of constitutional reform raises the second difficulty for the SNP: co-operation with other parties. Like all third parties, they have discovered that they have to make a choice between independence and getting things done. In 1989 the SNP made the crucial decision not to involve themselves in the Scottish Constitutional Convention, which included representatives of the churches, the trade unions and members of the European Parliament as well as Liberals and Labour. The reason was that the Convention was principally concerned with devolution, whereas the SNP would not concede anything short of independence. As a result relations have deteriorated to a point where many Labour supporters of a Scottish Parliament regard the SNP rather than the Conservatives as the main enemy, a reversion to the complaint that "Tartan Tories" brought down the Labour government in 1979. The SNP, for their part, are impatient with Labour's policy of NUNGE (Nothing Until the Next General Election), and the mutual hostility was made worse by the SNP's decision in the spring of 1993 to support the government in at least some aspects of the Maastricht Treaty rather than joining in opposition attempts to defeat the government. This decision also led to the resignation of three key SNP figures, and the leader, Alex Salmond, only narrowly survived a confidence motion. At the time of writing it is impossible to know how serious or permanent such a split might be.

All this creates the ironic situation that links have become closer between the SNP and the Tories than with Labour. Although John Major was decisive during the 1992 election campaign in his opposition to renegotiating the union with Scotland, he promised to "take stock" of the Scottish question. As well as the decision to hold the European Summit at the end of Britain's presidency in December 1992 in Edinburgh rather than London, there have been firm promises that more responsibilities will be devolved to the Scottish Office, amounting virtually to administrative devolution, an enhanced role for the Scottish Grand Committee and guaranteed representation for Scotland on the EC Committee of Regions, a promise which gained SNP support for Maastricht. Too close an alignment with the Conservatives would probably harm the SNP still further, but if they are looking to get what concessions they can short of independence, only the government can provide them.

The final danger for the SNP is that they may become irrelevant to the debate about the future of Scotland and the Union. The Scottish Constitutional Convention arose from pressure from the Campaign for a Scottish Assembly, and after the 1992 General Election there were several initiatives aimed at gaining a multi-choice referendum on the future. The most important of these is Scotland United, founded on the day after the General Election by George Galloway, John McAllion and Dennis Canavan. Among its supporters are pop musicians Pat Kane and Ricky Ross, and trade unionists such as Campbell Christie, General Secretary of the Scottish TUC. They claim 3 MEPs and 13 Scottish MPs, 6 of whom entered Parliament after 1989. In addition Scottish Militant is seen to be reviving, particularly in the form of the anti-poll tax campaigner Tommy Sheridan.

Clearly the SNP will have to make up its collective mind what to do. In general terms, there is a danger that the campaign for a referendum will fragment as the various groups squabble with each other, and constitutional solutions will be replaced by direct action, as Charles Gray, the Labour leader of Strathclyde Regional Council recommended shortly after the General Election. For the SNP, if they choose to remain in splendid isolation on the grounds that none of the other parties offers exactly what they want, they risk losing support as they have in the past.

16

Campaigns, advertising and opinion polls

Campaigning has been a part of the electoral scene since the later nineteenth century. The pattern was set by Gladstone's Midlothian campaigns of 1879 and 1880 when he toured his constituency attacking the government of Disraeli, oddly enough as a backbencher, having given up the leadership of the Liberal Party when defeated in 1874. In the 1945 General Election Attlee toured the country in a car driven by his wife. In 1951 Churchill, by then over 75, addressed meetings in Liverpool and Huddersfield within a week, returning to London between them. At the latter he spoke to 1,700 people, of whom 700 were Liberals. In 1959 Macmillan travelled 2,500 miles during the campaign and spoke at over 70 meetings, and in 1970 George Brown spoke to nearly 100 gatherings. All this was in addition to what was going on in individual constituencies.

Even as early as this, security considerations were affecting the freedom of campaigning in the old mode. When someone threw an egg at Harold Wilson, Edward Heath commented that since Wilson's itinerary was supposed to be secret, this must mean that there were people going about with eggs in their pockets on the off-chance of meeting the Prime Minister. Campaigning in 1974 was affected by the need to get the problems resolved in February, and the fact that nobody had anything new to say in October. By 1979 the danger of terrorism had further eroded the possibility of open mass meetings, and since then in general they have been replaced by all-ticket rallies where entrance can be carefully controlled, which is certainly safer, but less useful in stimulating political debate or in developing the skills necessary to cope with hecklers, which probably explains the generally low standard of debate in the House of Commons. In 1983 and 1987 the routes to be followed by the leaders were secret, but "photo-opportunities" were carefully staged, and in the case of Mrs Thatcher local managers and agents were told to have suitable crowds waiting. Only Michael Heseltine kept to the older style of campaigning, speaking in 108 constituencies in 1987, at his own expense, and in a vain attempt to regain favour. Under these conditions local party workers and even candidates were essentially agents of the national campaign, and often seemed to be getting in the way of it, in the perception of the voters. One candidate drew a picture of people sitting at home absorbing or modifying their political attitudes from the media, and regarding the visit of a canvasser as a tiresome distraction.

1992 may have seen a change. The rally held by Labour in Sheffield on 1 April was the ultimate in organisation and spectacle, but at best was a distraction from the issues, and at worst looked like counting chickens before they were hatched. John Major, by contrast, abandoned attempts at speaking to selected groups, particularly while gyrating on a bar-stool, in favour of a "soap-box", in the manner of his campaigns when he was a member of Lambeth Council. Whether it was a reversion to a more innocent age of campaigning, or only intended to look that way, it was an implicit criticism of the packaging attempted by the Conservatives' campaign managers. John Major virtually conceded as much when he told Edward Pearce that "it mattered finally being able to be me, and not somebody's idea of me". The most dismissive verdict was that of Austin Mitchell, who said that the national campaign was so boring that voters were actually happy to discuss issues at the door. The problems with the campaign for both major parties in 1992 may mean that there will be changes in approach next time.

Much of the change in campaigning in the last twenty years or so has been caused by the growing role of the media, and television in particular: in the words of Sundberg and Högnabba, "Free elections in a modern democracy would easily collapse if the mass media ... were to ignore election campaigning". As outlined in earlier chapters, the process began in 1955 when a group of ten newspaper editors interviewed members of the government, and developed steadily as more homes acquired TV sets, and gained an increasing amount of information from the screen rather than newspapers. As a result, parties and individuals made considerable efforts to project a more favourable image on the small screen, though many found the process of adaptation difficult, as can be seen from surviving examples of early election broadcasts.

Before long television was causing significant changes in the behaviour and apparent personality of major figures. In private life Harold Wilson preferred cigars, and spoke in the precise accent of an Oxford don, but for television he adopted a pipe and classless "northern" accents which had the added advantage that they were a gift to impressionists. Mrs Thatcher's career as leader of the Conservatives provides the most substantial and best-documented examples of the shaping of a British politician to the needs of television. Gordon Reece, a former TV producer who had advised Mrs Thatcher personally since 1970 and had written some of the 1974 election broadcasts became the party's Director of Communications in 1978, a full-time image-maker. Every aspect of Mrs Thatcher's image was assessed and altered where necessary, and great care was taken with the timing of interviews and the choice of interviewers: it was mainly Reece's decision to avoid a head-to-head confrontation in American style with Jim Callaghan in 1979. In spite of her often-expressed distrust of television and all its works, and her consistent opposition to televising the House of Commons, the greatest compliment that experienced television practitioners could find to pay Mrs Thatcher was that she handled the medium like an American. Opinion polls soon after the introduction of cameras to the Commons suggested that a majority believed Mrs Thatcher to be the most successful in adjusting to the new medium, even though Neil Kinnock was widely seen as a more skilled operator at the time of his election in 1983. John Major seemed less concerned with the problems of television, probably because he grew up with it, unlike Mrs Thatcher, and as suggested earlier, he eventually rebelled against attempts by the party managers to package him for television, particularly in ways which he felt did not suit him.

The 1992 campaign highlighted the way in which television has attempted to take over elections, rather than being only one of the means by which the parties present their policies: to adapt Marshall McLuhan, the medium has become more important than the message. The number of full-length interview programmes with leaders has risen steadily, seven in 1979, sixteen in 1983, for example. Both the BBC and ITN have adopted the American practice of assigning reporters and camera crews to specific individuals, while the parties in turn carefully monitor every programme dealing with the election, and reactions to each election broadcast, a pattern set by the Conservatives in 1983 and adopted by Labour in subsequent elections.

Often this has meant that the most notable events of a campaign are determined by television rather than simply being recorded by it. Thus in 1983 one of Mrs Thatcher's worst moments came when Mrs Diana Gould questioned her closely about the sinking of the *Belgrano* during the Falklands conflict, a clip frequently shown since. Both Denis Healey and Neil Kinnock were taking part in television discussions when their comments on Mrs Thatcher's attitude to the war aroused great controversy and did Labour no good. In 1987 Healey was involved in a public row about private health in a similar programme. Health was again the issue in the best-known example from 1992, the famous "Jennifer's ear" Labour Party broadcast. Instead of heightening voters' awareness of the problems of non-urgent surgery within the NHS, the broadcast provoked a dispute about itself, and the circumstances in which it was made. The Labour Party campaign manager responsible even felt obliged to defend herself at a subsequent press conference, so that the original issue effectively disappeared.

This episode illustrates the ability of television to eat its own children. Although television can heighten some issues, it cannot control the response, and there is well-established psychological evidence that viewers are looking to have their attitudes confirmed rather than altered. In 1966 when Edward Heath talked about remodelling the Welfare State, 48% of Conservatives thought he intended additional benefits to the needy and 31% more hospitals, whereas among Labour supporters 32% thought he was implying the restoration of prescription charges and 30% the re-introduction of means tests. The 1992 election broadcast mentioned above harmed both the major parties, and was seen as further evidence that neither could be trusted, the Conservatives because of their record on the Health Service, Labour because of their record on manipulative election management. It is true that surveys have shown that up to 70% of respondents regard television as their main source of political information, but the impact of individual broadcasts wears off very soon. In 1987 the "Kinnock" broadcast caused his personal rating to rise by 16 points for a few days, but there was very little impact on the final outcome, just as in 1992 the Conservatives particularly recovered from any harm done by Labour broadcasts.

The same questions about effectiveness apply to newspapers. In 1992 particularly there were claims that the tabloid newspapers had made a huge contribution to the success of the Conservatives, and Labour supporters have complained that British tabloids are the most biased of any Western democracy, and become more so in elections. The evidence is not conclusive, but suggests that readers treat newspapers with an even greater degree of scepticism than they do television: 70%–80% believe what they see or hear on radio and television, but only 40%–45% believe newspapers. Analysis of the political support of newspaper readers further undermines claims that they are totally decisive in determining how people vote (Table 16.1). What cannot be measured is the "water-torture" effect of the media. It has been claimed that Neil Kinnock has been a particular sufferer as he was consistently belittled as second-rate, and not competent to be Prime Minister. More recently a similar campaign in broadsheet newspapers targeted John Major, but it

Table 16.1   *Tabloid newspapers and political allegiance*

	1987		1992	
	Con.	*Lab.*	*Con.*	*Lab.*
The Sun	41	31	45	36
Daily Mirror	30	55	20	64
Daily Mail	60	13	65	15
Daily Express	70	9	67	15
Daily Star	28	46	31	54

is too soon to know whether this will be decisive in a future General Election.

There is a danger here. It is bad enough when the media trivialises political issues into "sound-bites" and the parties resort to "spin doctors" (the new piece of jargon from 1992) to process policies into a form acceptable to the media. There was very little attention paid to really significant issues in 1992, and a greater concentration on trivia and the processes of election management. In the first by-election of the new parliament, at Newbury in May 1993, around half the news stories were about media coverage, such as which senior figure was "minding" each candidate. Worse is the growing tendency of the media to ignore politics in favour of personalities, with the risk that British politics will go the way of American politics: that people will be deterred from entering public life, or will be unable to develop their careers because of the media spotlight on themselves and their families, a process seen in Britain with David Mellor, and in the United States in the difficulties Bill Clinton encountered in trying to find an Attorney-General. At about the same time a biography appeared of the Prime Minister's wife Norma, who very carefully kept herself and her family out of the public eye. Some idea of the change this represents can be gained by considering the likelihood of biographies appearing of Lady Churchill, Mrs Attlee or Lady Dorothy Macmillan while their respective husbands were Prime Minister. The second Calcutt enquiry in the autumn of 1992 suggested a need for more decisive curbs on media intrusion, and an implicit rejection of the standard media defence that people in public life must accept greater attention as a penalty of the job, and that news is whatever politicians want hidden.

At least this problem does not arise with the parties' own advertising, though that raises other important issues. The Conservatives were the first to use an advertising agency, under Harold Macmillan, and their best-known firm is Saatchi and Saatchi, used since 1979, though with varying degrees of success and approval: they have also been used by Conservatives in Denmark, Social Democrats in the Netherlands and Fianna Fail in Ireland. Political advertising is not only controversial by intent, it often arouses unintended controversies. Thus in 1970 Labour embarked on a two-part campaign contrasting "Yesterday's Men" (Conservatives) with the Labour future. Wilson's decision to call the election early meant that only the first part was seen, and the BBC adopted the title for a programme about Labour's defeat which infuriated Wilson. In 1979 there was argument over the Conservatives' use of actors and Young Conservatives in posters and "*vox pop.*" interviews, and in 1992 television and advertising frequently came together when the Conservatives launched a new topic by unveiling a poster on television.

One indirect question concerns the way in which the government since 1979 used advertising to project party policy. There are no constitutional problems when advertisements are presenting fairly neutral information on public health or road safety, but it was a different matter when the government sought to promote industries being prepared for privatisation, such as steel or water. There is a fairly thin dividing line between the government *informing* the electorate of the attractions of particular industries from a share-owning point of view, and *promoting* a policy likely to increase the share-owning classes who are liable to vote Conservative.

The most important question about advertising is the cost, and the associated issue of fairness to the parties. One of the oddities of our system is that there are no laws controlling *national* expenditure by parties, only that by individual candidates. Thus the amount spent by the major parties on their national campaign has soared since 1970 (though in real terms the Conservatives spent most in 1964), and most of this now goes on advertising. In 1983 the major parties spent more than half of their total expenditure centrally, and in 1987 the Conservatives spent at least £5 million of their central total of £9 million on national advertising, while Labour spent over half of their £4.7 million. The level of expenditure in 1987 enabled the Conservatives to take advertisements in all the national dailies in the last four days of the 1987 campaign and 217 pages in total, and Labour had 102 pages, compared with 17 pages for the Alliance.

This raises the question of the fairness of the funding available to the parties. In *Agenda for Change* (from which the above figures come) the argument is put forward that the differences between what the parties receive from their outside contributors are greatly reduced by the "benefits in kind" of free postage, rooms and television broadcasts, which they estimate amounted to £7.7 million in 1987. This is only true up to a point, as the figures indicate (Table 16.2).

Table 16.2   *Party spending, 1987 (figures from Agenda for Change)*

	Total spending	"Benefits in kind"	Spending less benefits
Conservative	£24.9m	£7.7m	£17.2m
Labour	£19.7m	£7.7m	£12.0m
Alliance	£16.5m	£7.7m	£8.7m

Thus the free postage and television formed nearly half the Alliance spending, but less than a third of Conservative spending. It is not surprising, therefore, to find that the Liberals argue strongly for state funding for parties both during and between elections, and for such aid to be linked to inflation. On the other hand the MORI survey commissioned by the Hansard Society in association with the report found only 39% in favour of state aid, and 53% against, but 80% in favour of limits on local spending and 81% of limits on national spending. Further work done on election management in general and on 1987 in particular suggests that effective dissemination of information about a party is related to the amount of resources and effort devoted to the campaign, but the evidence is not conclusive, and the 1992 campaign may show that the law of diminishing returns operates, in that beyond a certain point extra expenditure is wasted in terms of the improvement in vote share it produces.

Apart from spending on advertising, another area on which parties have spent considerable sums of money in recent campaigns has been opinion polls. Reflecting their straitened circumstances, the Liberals commissioned no private polls in 1987, and the SDP polled only about a dozen key marginals. By contrast the Conservatives used both Gallup and Harris, while Labour has had a long relationship with MORI. This is a far cry from the 1960s when Labour felt sufficiently safe to stop private polls for the 1966 election: now they are an integral part of campaigning, enabling parties to adapt their policy positions to the perceived mood.

The 1992 General Election revived the arguments about the reliability of opinion polls. As described in earlier chapters, they had a serious set-back in 1970. In May they were giving Labour a 7% lead, which helped to make up Wilson's mind on a June date, and though there were wide swings during the campaign, the polls were largely agreed on a comfortable Labour win, though probably with a reduced majority. In the event the Conservative lead was 3.4%, which the polls failed to detect, mainly because they stopped polling too early. The polls over-hauled their administration, and adopted a code of practice, and seemed to be justified by the result in February 1974, when the Conservatives had a lead of 1% in votes, though this was not translated accurately into seats, as the system worked in Labour's favour: during the campaign, as described in Chapter 6, the polls had accurately detected the leaching of support away from the major parties towards the Liberals. October 1974 was less successful for the polls, predicting a Labour lead of about 10% (a range from 4.5% to 14.5%), whereas Labour's own polls suggested 2.5% and a lead over the Conservatives of about 40 seats: in the event the lead was 42.

The period 1979–1987 saw the high point of the polls'

accuracy. In 1979 the Conservative lead fell from 10% at the start of the campaign to between 6% and 8%, close enough to the actual lead of 7%. In 1983 the polls were virtually unanimous in predicting a Conservative lead of at least 12%, and polls combined with computers to give a very accurate prediction of seats as soon as the polls closed, though as in the past, Alliance support was significantly underestimated. There was more disagreement in 1987, but as the figures in Chapter 10 show, the main parties were always within 5% of their standing at the start of the campaign, and the final figures were within 2%, an acceptable margin of error. As one veteran pollster said, the 1987 figures were much more typical of what the polls could achieve: for forecasts such as 1983 they need some luck as well.

There were fifty polls published between the calling of the 1992 election on 11 March and polling day on 9 April. Of these only six showed any sort of Conservative lead and, with the exception of a Harris poll taken between 21 and 23 March showing a Conservative lead of 5%, the largest advantage they had was 1%. Labour showed leads of 6–7% on several occasions, and though the exit polls were closer, as described in chapter 11, none of the polls matched the final Conservative lead of 7.6%. The pollsters were appalled, and launched an immediate enquiry into what had gone wrong. The findings were disconcerting. Late swing, as in 1970, under-registration in some constituencies to avoid the poll tax and the failure to include expatriate voters accounted for no more than half of the discrepancy between what the polls were showing and what happened. The remainder could only be explained by a consistent overestimate of Labour support probably as long as the polls had existed. Certainly whenever Labour had gone into a General Election with a clear poll lead, whether in 1964, 1966, 1970, October 1974 or 1992, they had performed markedly less well than the polls were indicating, and the only reason the problem had not been fully appreciated was that after 1974 Labour did not have a poll lead on the eve of a campaign.

The reason relates to a great extent to the manner in which

polls are taken, with pollsters questioning people either at random or more usually according to quotas of age, sex and class. It seems clear that of those who refuse to answer a substantial majority are Conservative supporters who either believe that it is no business of anybody's how they vote, or who are reluctant to give an answer which may not be "politically correct". This can also be seen in response to issues, as discussed in the next chapter.

Two questions arise from the performance of the polls in 1992: what is being done about it, and does it reinforce the claims that polls should be banned for all or part of a campaign? The answer to the first question is not easy, since there is no guaranteed way to be sure that a respondent is giving a reliable answer. One solution is to use more open questions such as "Which party are you more inclined to vote for?"; another is to use secret ballots. Whether either will be successful in bringing the polls back to their perceived levels of accuracy in the 1980s will not be known for certain until the next General Election. In response to the second question, only 21% of the MORI survey believed that polls should be banned, and the report commented that in France, where the publication of polls is forbidden in the last week of the campaign, there is simply a great deal of speculation based on the polls which have not been published. Some idea of the impact if this were to happen here may be gained from the realisation that a week before polling day in 1992 Labour had a lead of 2–3%. The polls provide parties with information on the key issues, and voters with help in making up their minds. The 1992 result has reminded pollsters that politics is about people, not arithmetical units. If they, the media which publishes polls and the campaign managers who interpret them can respond, then 1992 may turn out to have done some good for the British electoral system after all.

17
Voting behaviour

Psephology, the systematic analysis of voting behaviour, is a post-war phenomenon, like election analysis in general; from investigating how people vote, it was a small step to considering what might influence the way they vote. In the same way that the electoral system was assumed to work in fairly simple and predictable ways, as discussed in Chapter 1, psephologists believed that there was a simple and predictable set of influences on the vast majority of voters. Most people, perhaps as many as 85%, always voted in the way they had at first, and their first decision was largely determined by their social class, which in turn was mainly determined by that of their parents. Any other factors affecting voting preferences, such as age, sex or religion, could be explained in class terms. Thus as people aged, they would move away from abstention or third parties to the major parties, and as they increased in responsibilities such as home ownership they would move to the Conservatives. If a family moved, the wife was likely to be affected by the new surroundings, whereas the husband might still be at the same place of work, and women were in general more likely to vote Conservative. Catholics were likely to be mainly working class and thus to support Labour. Almost any figures could be quoted to emphasise the close links between social class and voting in the years after 1945, and those of the 1970 General Election make the point as well as any (Table 17.1).

Even the number of C2 and DE (working-class) voters

Table 17.1 *Voting allegiance by social class, 1970*

	AB	C1	C2	DE
Conservative	79	59	35	32
Labour	10	31	55	57

supporting the Conservatives was explained by "deference", the voters' belief that the Conservatives were the best suited by ability and experience to govern. This was assumed to be uniform, and therefore another aspect of class-based voting.

The results in 1974 appeared to continue the post-war trend, and any weakening in support for the major parties was assumed at the time to be caused by the electorate's loss of confidence in them and the consequent rise in Liberal support (Table 17.2).

Table 17.2 *Voting allegiance by social class, 1974 (average)*

	AB	C1	C2	DE
Conservative	65	51	28	23
Labour	11	23	48	56
Liberal	21	23	20	16

The 1979 results showed that there had been a further reduction of 'traditional' support for both the major parties, suggesting that even in 1974 the bonds between parties and classes were beginning to weaken, and this trend has largely been confirmed by subsequent results. By 1992 Conservative middle class support was down to 56% (AB) and 52% (C1); Labour's working class support reached its nadir in 1983 (32% C2, 41% DE) and was still below the 1974 figures in 1992 (40% C2, 48% DE according to Gallup, 55% DE according to Harris) (Figure 17.1).

As already discussed in Chapters 12 and 13, this "class de-alignment" has been matched by "partisan de-alignment" as the bonds between supporters and parties have become weaker. Academic studies, particularly those carried out in the early 1980s suggest between any two elections up to one-third of voters will change their minds, over three elections the proportion

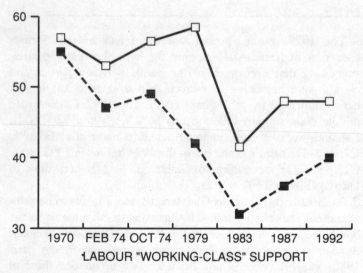

Fig. 17.1 Party support from "traditional" classes, 1970–1992

rises to 40% and over four may be as high as a half. Once a voter has changed he/she is likely to change again, and the clear message from opinion polls is that many more voters think about changing their vote than actually do it. Between 1979 and 1983 the Conservatives lost 32% of their vote, the Liberals 39% and Labour 46%: between 1983 and 1987 the figures were 23%, 30% and 25% respectively. Even in 1987 nearly one-fifth of voters were still undecided at the start of the campaign, and in 1992 this was over a quarter, with a majority of those leaving their choice to the last few days.

It is not possible to give definite reasons for this increased volatility on the part of voters. One possible reason is "embourgeoisement", the process of becoming middle class, as Ivor Crewe's analysis has implied. Another possible explanation is much greater information and education on politics, enabling voters to make a more informed, less automatic decision. Richard Rose summed this up in the title of a book written in the heyday of the Alliance, *Voters Begin to Choose*.

Now that it is clear that the old explanations are no longer complete, recent analysis has understandably concentrated on the factors which may have replaced class as the main determinants of voting behaviour. Although psephologists still disagree, the accumulated evidence of the latest General Elections has enabled a clearer picture to emerge.

Issue voting.

Issues rather than social factors have always played a major part in by-elections, and analysts are now broadly agreed that most voters make up their minds on issues in General Elections as well. Issue voting apparently takes two forms, the general and the personal, sometimes known as "secular" voting. According to its advocates, the first involves voters identifying the most important issues and voting for the party which is seen as the strongest on them: thus people are likely to support Labour if they regard health or welfare as the most significant issues, the Conservatives if they are more influenced by defence or law and order.

This analysis is open to considerable criticism. In the first place many voters find difficulty in knowing which party supports which policy, assuming that there is any clear difference: in 1987, for example, over half those questioned did not know which party most strongly supported proportional representation at the time. Elections since 1970 have shown that it is impossible for any group, politicians or media, to define the agenda in terms of issues. In February 1974 the question "who rules, government or unions?" was uppermost in Edward Heath's mind when he called the General Election, but before long wages and prices took over as the main concern of the electorate, leading to a loss of support for both major parties. More recently, Labour's attempts in 1992 to focus on health, through their "Jennifer's Ear" broadcast, merely succeeded in confusing the issue.

The issue theory of voting behaviour has suffered more damage from the elections of 1987 and 1992. In 1987 at least 75% of the electorate saw health, unemployment and education as the most important issues, and had Labour ahead on them by anything from 12% to 27%, yet the Conservatives had a winning margin of nearly 12%. Clearly, to adapt George Orwell, some issues were more equal than others, and attention needed to be given to the salience of issues as well as the position of the parties. The 1992 election confirmed this: for example 41% mentioned the National Health Service and hospitals as the most important issue, 36% unemployment and 23% education, as against 11% mentioning prices and 10% taxation, but when it came to deciding, the Conservatives surged ahead on economic issues while Labour declined on welfare (see Table 11.2 for the detailed figures).

This has led some observers to analyse voting behaviour entirely in terms of individual selfishness, a criticism frequently levelled at Thatcherism in general. As long ago as 1861 John Stuart Mill pointed out that "a man's interest consists of whatever he takes an interest *in* ... A selfish man will prefer even a trifling individual benefit to his share of the advantage which his country would derive from a good law: because interests peculiar to himself are those which the habits of his mind both dispose him to dwell on and make him best able to estimate" ("*Considerations on Representative Government*," Ch. X). Clearly the success of Conservative attacks on Labour's taxation plans in 1987 and 1992 offer some support for this belief, as does Ivor Crewe's analysis of new and old working class, but once again there is room for doubt. Support for the Conservatives from owner occupiers has shown a steady fall, from 47% in 1983 to 44% in 1987 and 40% in 1992. More fundamentally it has been shown that in February 1974 and 1979 General Elections were held after sharp increases in income and consumption which had left the majority of voters markedly better off than they had been a year earlier: the government lost. In 1983 and 1992 the elections were held during or just after the worst periods of recession since the Second World War, and the government still won, by a landslide in 1983, unexpectedly in 1992. Admittedly there were many factors involved, but voters were clearly influenced by their belief that one party was more likely to guarantee continued prosperity than the other.

Perceived Competence.

Voters' confidence in the ability of a government to deliver has been variable. In the 1970s there was a strong belief that all governments were incapable of carrying out their intentions. One reason was the general failure of Labour and Conservative governments to implement their election promises; indeed they seemed at times to be making a virtue of changing with every circumstance, on the principle that changing your mind implies that you are wiser today than you were yesterday. There were more general explanations, usually lumped together under the term "overload". Put simply, this argued that voters' expectations of government were increasing at the same time that the capacity of government to satisfy those expectations was being restricted, partly by factors which they could not control, such as oil prices, partly by their need to work in partnership with a variety of interests which had the power to disrupt or destroy government policy if it did not suit them. This was a particular problem with attempts to introduce an organised pay policy in the 1970s.

"Thatcherism" was a deliberate attack on this perception: the twin weaknesses of consensus and corporatism could easily be cured by a strong dose of conviction. There is no doubt that this was a definite asset in 1983 and 1987: the Conservatives were likely to carry out their promises, whereas Labour would be the prisoner of their past and the unions, and the Alliance would not win enough seats. To a certain extent this was still the attitude in 1992, with Labour still unable to convince the electorate that their policies would work, or that they could fulfil them.

Either side of the 1992 General Election the Conservative image became severely dented. Between 1987 and 1990 sharp rises in inflation, interest rates and unemployment, followed by the shambles of the community charge and a spate of resignations ("spending more time with the family" almost became a code for "getting out while the going was good") created a strong impression that the government's insistence on following its convictions was doing more harm than good, and particularly was jeopardising its chances of winning the next election. As described earlier, this led directly to the challenge to Mrs Thatcher's leadership. The fifteen months after the 1992 victory saw a vertiginous decline in Conservative fortunes to the lowest point since surveys began even though all the economic factors were favourable: inflation and unemployment were falling steadily and output and confidence were rising. In spite of this, the government was seen as having lost its way, confirming the belief among many psephologists that the electorate does not greatly mind what a government does so long as it does something.

Image: leaders and candidates.

Since 1945 there has frequently been a contradiction between the image of the party and the image of the leader. In 1945 Churchill was far more highly regarded than Attlee, yet Labour won by a landslide. In 1970 Wilson, "the best Conservative Prime Minister around" lost to the little-regarded Heath, and the same happened in 1979 with Callaghan and Thatcher: in each case voters supported the party in spite of their lukewarm enthusiasm for its leader. In many ways this was true of the whole of the Thatcher period. In 1981 and 1985 she was seen as an electoral liability by many, and in 1989 a Gallup survey on her ten years in office found that she was respected by 67% but disliked by 63%, nearly as many. Far more saw her as out of touch with ordinary people in 1989 than in 1979, and her departure in 1990 saw a surge in support for the Conservative Party as a whole as well as for John Major. His image was clearly a positive factor in the Conservative success in 1992, indeed it could have made the difference between winning and losing, but after that it rapidly became a liability. By the summer of 1993 less than 16% regarded him as the best Prime Minister either actual or potential.

Labour has generally found the image of the leader to be a problem rather than an asset, apart from the victories by Harold Wilson in 1964 and 1966. In 1983 the party's divisions were amplified by the weak image of Michael Foot: in 1987 the attempts by the party's image-makers to play the Conservatives at their own game by projecting Neil Kinnock as a personality rather than as party leader did not work: 44% regarded him as the worst possible Prime Minister against 31% believing him the best. In 1992 he was even more of a liability, with only 28% at most regarding him as the best potential Prime Minister, and only 21% by polling day, against 51% considering him the worst choice. The image of a divided leadership clearly cost the Alliance dearly in 1987, and even in 1992 Paddy Ashdown's support was less than 20%, but after that his stock rose steadily: by mid-1993 nearly a quarter saw him as the best possible Prime Minister, when John Major's support was under 16%.

The image of individual candidates has probably been more important in by-elections than General Elections, and so should perhaps be seen as an aspect of protest: the Conservative loss of Eastbourne and their failure to take Bradford North were both blamed on an unwise choice of candidate. In General Elections voters are more prepared to overlook the shortcomings of an individual in their enthusiasm for a party, since our electoral system makes such a choice necessary. In 1992, however, there was the unfortunate instance of John Taylor, whose selection as Conservative candidate for Cheltenham provoked great argument, either because of his colour or because he was a London-based barrister. Whatever the reason, the seat was lost, with a swing from Conservative to Liberal of more than 5%. Whatever the personal qualities of a candidate, voters clearly now expect a much greater involvement by their candidates in constituency affairs, and responsibility for national campaigning has not been enough to save prominent figures from defeat, as Shirley Williams found in 1979 and Chris Patten in 1992.

Demographic factors: geography and race

In the heyday of "class-based" psephology, geography and race were assumed to be glosses on social class. Scotland was the only area to show a significant swing to Labour in the period 1959–1983, but this was assumed to be caused by a higher than average proportion of manual workers. Even then, there was room for doubt: in Scotland 50% of manual workers supported Labour, but in the South only 25% did so. In 1983 and 1987 there was a clear north-south divide in voting patterns, but in 1992 the picture was less clear. Conservative support rose in Scotland (by 1.7%) and the north of England (by 0.5%) but fell elsewhere, by over 1% in the Midlands and the south. Labour support fell in Scotland (by 3.4%), but rose everywhere else, by 6.3% in the Midlands and 4.3% in the south. Thus the pattern of the previous elections, that both major parties increased their vote where they were already strong, was not maintained, and there is still no firm evidence that where people live actually influences the way they vote, especially if they move.

Little attention has been given to the voting behaviour of ethnic minorities until recently. In 1964, when race and immigration first became significant electoral issues, virtually all immigrant groups felt alienated from British politics: only a minority voted, and many were not even registered. Over subsequent General Elections it was clear that an overwhelming proportion of ethnic minority voters supported Labour: 81% in October 1974, 86% in 1979. This led to the assumption that this was determined by a single set of factors which were probably little different from those affecting others of their class (predominantly unskilled manual or unemployed): even more than for white voters, unemployment was seen as the most important issue, and there were few signs that minorities had gained much from any increase in prosperity in the 1980s.

Table 17.3   *Party support by ethnic minorities*

	Afro-Caribbean	Asian
1983		
Labour	87	81
Conservative	7	8
Alliance	5	10
1987		
Labour	86	67
Conservative	6	23
Alliance	7	10

Though there is little evidence available at the moment from the 1992 General Election, it seems probable that the ethnic vote is becoming more complex, and that it should certainly not be seen as monolithic. The first line of division is between Afro-Caribbeans and Asians, with the former remaining far more loyal to Labour than the latter (Table 17.3). Thus there was a swing of 14.5% from Labour to Conservative among Asian voters. Asians were also more likely to vote: in 1987 a survey found that 74% said they were certain to vote against only 51% Afro-Caribbeans, reviving the argument that disappointed Labour voters are more likely to abstain. The Asian vote is itself divided: there is evidence that Asians from East Africa, who came to Britain from Kenya and Uganda in the late 1960s and early 1970s are more ready to support the Conservatives than those from the Indian sub-continent. In areas where there is a relatively low concentration of immigrants the proportion not voting Labour may be more than half, as against less than a quarter in areas of high immigrant density.

The 1992 General Election showed that ethnic minorities are responding to issues: as Mihir Bose put it just before the election, Asians "are beginning to show the sense of discrimination and scepticism which distinguishes the rest of the British electorate." One particularly sensitive issue between Indians and Pakistanis has been the future of Kashmir, and Asian voters were also influenced by the Salman Rushdie affair, the question of separate Muslim schools–as part of the increasing assertion and defence of traditional Muslim values against the influence of the West–and the impact of the failure of the Bank of Credit and Commerce International.

This is important for Labour. As Bose pointed out in the same article, if every Muslim who voted Labour in 1987 switched to the Conservatives, they would certainly lose some seats, and could fall short of forming a government. With the voting picture becoming ever more volatile, and the margin between the major parties narrowing, every vote, and the influences determining it, is vital.

Protest and tactical voting

Negative forms of voting, which these are, have been more commonly seen in by-elections when less is at stake, but they are clear evidence of the weakening of the traditional bonds between voters and the political processes. Between 1987 and 1992 the Conservatives lost over 20% of their 1987 vote in four by-elections, winning only one: Labour lost nearly 28% at Govan and the Liberals lost at least 10% in two by-elections. The Conservative loss of support had to do mainly with issues such as the poll tax and the Health Service, and indirectly with the image of Mrs Thatcher: image was the determining factor in the by-elections after the 1992 election. Labour and the Liberals suffered from an unfavourable image, either of weak opposition or of internal weaknesses. Every seat lost by the Conservatives and Labour before 1992 was regained in the

General Election, confirming that voters will protest when they are not choosing a government, but will revert to their previous allegiance if there is a danger of another party coming to power.

The same is true of tactical voting: the belief that the party a voter supports cannot win, so the vote is cast to defeat the party most disliked. A survey in June 1987 for the Hansard Society found that only 9% of those expressing an opinion would vote tactically: even among Liberal supporters it was only 15%.

A new psephology?

The disappearance of traditional features of the voting landscape in the 1970s has already forced analysts to find new explanations. The 1992 General Election made the scene even more confused, particularly in the field of "swing". Instead of being uniform, this varied from region to region and even from seat to seat. In the south-east the "average" swing from Conservative to Labour was 6% and from Conservative to Liberal 4.5%. Taking three adjacent constituencies shows the degree of variability: in Dover there was a swing of 5.2% from Conservative to Labour; in Folkestone and Hythe 0.6% from Conservative to Liberal; and in Ashford 0.7% from Liberal to Conservative. Even if the constitutional framework remains unchanged, which is unlikely, as discussed in the final chapter, there will be a need for a more localised psephology, with analysts concentrating much more on what happens in individual constituencies and much less on overall trends which have become increasingly misleading in recent years. If subsequent General Elections confirm the de-constructing trends of 1992 it may be impossible to write about voting behaviour in any general sense at all.

18

The impact of elections

For much of the 1970s the theory of "overload" discussed in the previous chapter was believed to extend to elections: Richard Rose summed this up in the question "Do parties make a difference?" The factors which governments could not control, the influence of civil servants and the similarity of the parties' policies meant that it made little difference which party was in power: winning or losing thus became irrelevant to the way the country was governed, and voters were faced with a difference of styles rather than fundamentals. During the 1980s the Conservative governments under Mrs Thatcher attacked all the assumptions of the post-war consensus, insisting that governments should do what they believe to be right, and not be deflected by any outside forces. This meant that the unions, civil servants and local government were not only ignored, they were subject to a series of changes designed to prevent them from playing a decisive role in the future. Thus the 1979 General Election was seen as a watershed in post-war British political history comparable only with 1945. More recently, and particularly since Mrs Thatcher's fall in 1990, this assumption has been questioned from several viewpoints, and most analysts would no longer give a dogmatic answer to Rose's question.

Elections certainly still matter in the constitutional, liberal democratic sense. In *The Social Contract* Jean-Jacques Rousseau argued that England was most truly a democracy in elections, since voters were free to get rid of their rulers in a way denied in more authoritarian regimes. The most effective way, perhaps the only way, in which governments can be held accountable is the fear of losing office: this is the reason for the calls during the nineteenth century for more frequent elections, such as the Chartists' demand for annual parliaments. Even if voters do not wish to get rid of the existing government, or are reluctant to entrust power to one of the alternatives, elections focus their attention on political processes and issues to an extent which is rare otherwise. If anyone doubts the degree of interest generated by elections, even among those who cannot yet vote, the Hansard Society/Newsround Mock Election in 1992 provides ample evidence, with up to half a million schoolchildren campaigning and voting.

The right to stand for Parliament is an important aspect of citizenship: not only are candidates guaranteed free postage and hire of rooms, they are certain to get attention, particularly in by-elections. At the Christchurch by-election in the summer of 1993 there were fourteen candidates, several concentrating on one specific policy issue, such as the future of the European Community. In 1981 the IRA hunger striker Bobby Sands took advantage of a legal loophole to stand and to be elected: in 1990 a National Health Party was set up by a group of doctors to protest about changes in the NHS. In a lighter vein, "Lord" David Sutch, Britain's longest serving party leader, has based his entire career on this constitutional right.

For the parties elections have proved vital, in policies, leadership and structure. The Conservatives adjusted their policies to the implications of the 1945 General Election and the work of the Labour government, accepting a mixed economy and a wide-ranging welfare system, and maintained their policies through the 1950s and 1960s. Before the 1970 election they carried out a thorough reappraisal, prompting jibes about "Selsdon Man", and a flirtation with "Thatcherism" which was halted by the belief that growth was more important than monetary discipline. The Conservative style of government from 1972 to 1974 was little different from the Labour governments before and afterwards. After 1974 a new leader meant a new approach which only became apparent after the Conservatives' return in 1979. The Conservative leadership has more often than not been determined by electoral considerations. Churchill and Thatcher were persuaded to go because they were likely to lose the next election, as, arguably, was Macmillan. Douglas-Home and Heath were removed because they had already lost, and were thought unlikely to win in future. Even when they have won, the Conservative organisation has been criticised, most recently in 1987 and 1992, resulting in a major overhaul: in 1992 the costs of the Conservative campaign led to substantial job losses at Central Office which were only incidentally caused by the alleged defects of the campaign.

Labour's response to election defeats began in 1979 when the party moved sharply to the left, a route also followed by the two nationalist parties. The changes were fundamental, in policies, in leadership and in procedures. After 1983 there were some changes in style, but a more fundamental change in the decision to proceed against Militant, which recalled some of Labour's internal disputes before the Second World War. Outside the House of Commons some Labour supporters took the view that parliamentary opposition was a waste of time, and that the main challenge to the government had to come from local government, such as the GLC, Liverpool and Lambeth, and the unions, notably the NUM in 1984/1985. This might have represented a significant constitutional shift in the direction of extra-parliamentary opposition if it had had support from the party leadership and if it had worked. After the 1987 election the changes were more fundamental: policies traditional in the Labour Party since 1918 were amended almost out of existence; many of the principles of the market and other features of Thatcherism were accepted; and many of the organisational changes of the 1980s were called into question. After the 1992 election the process continued, with arguments about constitutional and electoral reform, discussed in the next chapter, and radical new proposals for taxation. It is legitimate to argue that none of this would have happened, certainly not to such an extent, without the succession of election defeats suffered by Labour since 1979.

The same argument applied to the Alliance. Its formation owed little or nothing to election results, and presumably the Liberals would have been happy to continue as they had done since the war and continued to do after the merger with most of the SDP. On the other hand the break-up of the Alliance was undoubtedly the result of two disappointing performances in General Elections and particularly the problems revealed in the 1987 campaign, though several analysts of parties have shown that the Alliance held the seeds of its own destruction from the beginning and would probably have fallen apart at some stage even if it had been more electorally successful.

If elections have clearly had a considerable effect on the operation and fortunes of the parties, their effect on the country as a whole is much more debatable. The most potent advocacy for the importance of elections come from those analysts who see 1979 as a watershed: once the Conservatives had come to power they set about dismantling all the key features of the post-war consensus, replacing it by their own attitudes and assumptions with which Labour has had to come to terms in their search for victory. Thus the unions, "appeased" by Labour and Conservative alike in the 1950s saw immunities dating back to the early years of the century swept away during the 1980s by successive legislation. Local government, the chosen instrument of much social policy after the war in the fields of health, housing and education came under attack in two ways. Centrally-imposed policies such as the sale of council houses, the establishment of Housing Action Trusts, Local Management of schools and the National Curriculum removed many of local government's traditional responsibilities, while rate-capping, the community charge and the council tax reduced the scope of local authorities to raise revenue and gave central government an increased control over the purse-strings. By the time of the next General Election it is probable that at least one level of local government will have disappeared in many parts of the country. The Civil Service, which assumed that it would be trusted by Conservatives even if Labour governments were traditionally suspicious, saw the Civil Service Department killed off in 1981 and departments and agencies being "privatised" under the "Next Steps" programme. Morale slumped in the Civil Service as they saw themselves being relegated to mere administration of policies decided by politicians and advisers, without the help which Civil Servants regarded it as their main function to provide.

Even in 1987 it was possible to question the view of 1979 as a decisive turning-point in Britain's post-war political development, and after 1990 it was more difficult than ever to believe that the British political scene had been transformed by the innovatory power of political will combined with a radical ideology. In the first place, many of the changes associated with Thatcherism had been prefigured long before. The first post-war attempt to bring the unions within a framework of legal constraints was Harold Wilson's "In Place of Strife" ten years before the first "Thatcherite" act, and Edward Heath's Industrial Relations Act of 1971 confirmed the difficulties, it did not create them. The Conservative legislation since 1980 is different in degree, not in kind. It was a Labour minister, Anthony Crosland, who told the local authorities soon after reorganisation in 1974 that "the party's over", meaning that levels of spending by the newly-amalgamated authorities were unacceptable to the government in view of the prevailing economic situation. The attack on the Civil Service began with the Fulton Committee whose report appeared in 1969, and though the 1977 Select Committee investigation of the Civil Service decided that the Fulton recommendations were dead, the assumptions were clearly revived by the post-1979 Conservative governments. One assumption was that the Civil Service would always try to freeze out change: the consequence would be that radical change would only be achieved by neutralising or marginalising the Civil Service, even if it involved taking much of the machinery of government out of the hands of the Civil Service altogether. The Fulton reforms would probably have created a Civil Service similar to that existing in the 1990s if they had been implemented at the time.

It is also legitimate to ask whether the impact of Thatcherism has affected the way people think about the main features of the post-war consensus. Certainly most people have accepted the changes outlined above, as well as the changes in education, but the welfare state is a different matter: there is clear evidence that people are content with the National Health Service in particular, and are very reluctant to see changes which would harm its capacity to deliver the service they want. Thus in 1989–1990 ambulance drivers attracted great support during their six-month dispute from a public which, to paraphrase the legendary Quaker, not only felt for them, it felt in its pocket: some ambulance stations raised enough in voluntary donations to pay most of their staff. The changes proposed in the 1989 NHS Review affecting calculation of funding and providing the opportunity for major hospital to "opt out" of local control met with great opposition: concerns about the fate of a local hospital clearly contributed to the Conservative loss in the Monmouth by-election.

Mrs Thatcher was ousted soon afterwards, and events after her fall in 1990 cast further doubt on the permanence of the "Thatcher revolution" apparently begun with the 1979 election victory. Some things did not change, of course: the programmes in education, local government organisation and the Civil Service continued unabated, for example. Some of the changes were differences in style. John Major's emphasis on "a nation at ease with itself" initially looked attractive after the increasingly strident character of the later Thatcher years, but as discussed in Chapter 12 the style came to look indecisive and lacking any sense of direction, particularly in the difficulties over Europe.

This has been reflected in the number of changes of policy since 1990. The first, to nobody's regret, was the abandonment of the poll tax, in spite of (or perhaps because of) Mrs Thatcher's description of it as the flagship of her government's third term. With hindsight, it was significant that the impact of the poll tax was mitigated by the raising of VAT to $17\frac{1}{2}\%$, since many of the main components of economic Thatcherism have disappeared. The decision to shadow the Deutschmark and then to enter the Exchange Rate Mechanism, both of which happened before Mrs Thatcher fell, could be justified as part of an anti-inflation policy, but after 1992 both public spending and government borrowing were allowed to grow at a rate that would horrify monetarists, and many within the party favoured increasing taxes, particularly VAT, rather than cutting public spending.

Economic policy is particularly relevant to elections because so many voters are influenced by their perception of the government's ability to control the economy. Yet most of the changes in economic attitudes have been independent of elections: indeed politics and the economy often seem to be moving on independent tracks, and if they collide there is usually damage to one or the other. The policies followed after the 1970 election were aimed at keeping the money-supply under control in order to keep inflation down, but the U-turn of 1972 saw spending and growth emphasised instead, with inflation set on an upward trend which did not end until the early 1980s. Many believe that the revival of monetarism came not in 1979 but in 1976 when the International Monetary Fund insisted on tight curbs on the money supply as a condition of help.

Revision of the post-war consensus view of unemployment came even earlier. The Keynesian view was that full employment, defined as 97% of the work-force, could either be achieved naturally or, if not, through government intervention in the labour market through a mixed economy. This seemed to work during the 1940s and early 1950s, which may have lulled governments into a false sense of security, particularly about the efficiency of the welfare state. But by the late 1950s successive Chancellors of the Exchequer were warning that 3% unemployment might be unrealistic, and that the economy might need to be run at a higher level of joblessness. The need to bring inflation down, after 1979 and after 1990, resulted in a massive rise in unemployment, and the level in the first quarter of 1990, 5.7%, was the lowest for ten years. Although unemployment showed small and unexpected (not to say inexplicable) falls in the first half of 1993 it was still way above the 1990 level. After the 1987 election it looked as though the same argument might apply to inflation, that it could not be kept below 5% for very long except at the cost of a massive squeeze on wages and borrowing. Inflation rates in 1993, both headline and underlying, were the lowest for many years, and well within the government's targets, but how long this could continue in view of the size of the government's borrowing commitments and the fragile state of business confidence was a question to which nobody had a reliable answer.

This raises the fundamental question: can governments manage the economy at all, or is the electorate's confidence misplaced? Certainly governments place great reliance on their ability to control economic change, but the evidence is very far from conclusive. During the "Butskell" era of the 1950s, when there was broad consensus on the aims and methods of economic measurement, high interest rates were regarded with horror, and pressure of demand was regulated by fiscal means, usually some time after the event, hence the derisive description "stop-go". More often than not problems were sorting themselves out, and government action made things worse. In the period from 1964 the pound/dollar exchange rate followed a cycle covering roughly four and a half years, rising between 1968 and 1972, falling from 1972 to 1976 irrespective of the government in power and their views on the value or otherwise of fixed exchange rates. Output was better in the decade from 1979 than in the decade before, but worse than in the 1950s and 1960s. Taxation provides at least the same proportion of national income as in 1979, and public spending is roughly the same proportion of output. The large budget surpluses built up during the 1980s were allowed to shrink in the 1990s: for example in the first ten months of the financial year 1989/1990 the surplus fell by nearly half. After that the impact of recession meant that it was impossible for government to plan for any surplus at all. Perhaps the strongest argument for the fundamental impotence of governments in managing the economy lies in the fact that the greatest difficulties in the 1990s resulted from German reunification and the response to economic pressures by the Bundesbank. It is difficult for governments to sound convincing when they claim that entry to an Exchange Rate Mechanism is vital to economic health, as in 1990, and that leaving it is equally vital, as in 1992. It goes without saying that if the impotence of governments in controlling the economy in general is accepted, they are unlikely to be able to manipulate economic factors to help in winning an election. Even if they try, they cannot guarantee that the benefits will last.

Although economic competence is probably the main issue influencing voters, it is clearly not the only one: but if issues determine voting preference, then this provides further evidence for the relative irrelevance of elections. The parties cannot control the way in which issues become prominent during a campaign. In February 1974 the Conservatives could not keep the collective mind of the electorate focused on the unions; and in 1992 Labour could not prevent the issues of the health service raised by their 'Jennifer's Ear' broadcast being more concerned with mechanics than principles.

Even if issues are not confused by the way in which the parties handle them, there is often no real choice for the electorate. Europe is particularly revealing in this respect. In 1970 and the two elections of 1974 all the major parties supported Britain's membership: in 1992 all the parties favoured the development of the European Community implied by the Maastricht Treaty. In each case the differences were marginal: in each case voters who opposed the prevailing attitude had no one for whom to vote. The view put forward in old-fashioned textbooks that great questions are decided by General Elections is now totally discredited: either the parties do not disagree on the major questions, or do not wish to jeopardise votes by supporting a minority view.

Even more serious is the claim that General Elections do not concern themselves with the most important issues, preferring to concentrate on marginal or parochial questions. As well as the future development of the European Community, whether by expansion or future integration of political or economic systems, such issues as the combination of a falling birth-rate and a falling death-rate (the so-called "demographic time-bomb"), the environment and the spread of such diseases as Aids did not figure significantly among the policies of the major parties at any time during the post-war period. Where they did occur, as when the Conservatives "adopted" the Green agenda in 1988, it was more for party advantage than as a response to public concern. Since pressure groups need to rely on luck or political or economic leverage to make an impact, there is a danger that a gulf will develop between electorate and government even during General Elections, let alone between them, so that elections, far from being the main guarantee of governmental accountability, will be irrelevant to Britain's political processes and the real needs of the electorate.

19

The constitutional future

The question of reforming Britain's political structures and processes has appeared in General Elections only spasmodically. It was, perhaps, implicit in the election of 1945, but the changes involved in joining the European Community were almost totally ignored in 1970. In 1974 Labour proposed to hold a referendum once they had re-negotiated the terms of membership, but in the prevailing economic situation this made little difference to the attitudes of most voters. The 1979 General Election gave a verdict on the proposals for devolution in Scotland and Wales, though only as part of a general loss of confidence in the government, and thereafter constitutional change formed no part of any party's appeal in 1983 and 1987.

By 1992 the question of Britain's constitution had become much more prominent. Pressure groups such as Charter 88 argued that the basic rights of the citizen had been steadily and deliberately eroded over the previous ten years. These rights needed to be restored, but in addition safeguards needed to be installed to ensure that they could not be infringed in such a way again. This would almost certainly mean changes to the structure and processes of British politics, not just a written constitution or Bill of Rights which governments could ignore in the same way that they have ignored the "checks and balances" of the present unwritten system. In the 1992 election the apparently very small margin between the parties throughout the campaign led to discussion of constitutional development to an extent not seen since 1974: specifically the question of what would happen if there were to be a hung parliament, both immediately and in the longer term.

It is not the purpose of this chapter to discuss the general question of the rights of the citizen, but to consider the more limited question of possible changes which might affect the electoral system or the outcome of elections. The most drastic, and therefore the least likely, would be the introduction of regular referendums. There were particularly strong demands for this from Lady Thatcher and other opponents during the debates on the Maastricht Treaty, and the introduction of popular votes on issues of major importance would certainly resolve the difficulties discussed in the previous chapter.

Past experience is not encouraging. In 1974 Labour's promise to hold a referendum was the result of a Cabinet split and the need to present some sort of alternative to the Conservatives: in any case Harold Wilson was confident that he would win. The referendums held in 1979 on Scottish and Welsh devolution were introduced as a time-bomb by opponents of devolution against the wishes of a government which was too weak to resist. There was no serious intention to consult the electorate on an issue of major constitutional importance, indeed the possibility of a referendum on the subject in *England* was never seriously considered: these referendums were purely tactical. A government will not hold a referendum unless it is sure that it will win, when it does not need to. Unless a referendum is binding, the government can ignore the result, as Labour might have done in Scotland if they had won in 1979. Much depends on the way in which the question is framed. There is also the danger of "participation fatigue". In Switzerland a referendum must be held at local, cantonal or national level if requested by a certain number of voters, but all too often they attract a low turnout made up of the committed on one side or the other.

Labour's decision to introduce devolution legislation after 1974 was partly motivated by the need to guarantee the support of the nationalist parties, and the same could happen again. If Scotland and Wales were to be granted elected assemblies this

could have important consequences for the British electoral
system. Representation would be a particular problem. If Scotland
and Wales kept their guaranteed number of MPs, this would
create the strange situation that Scottish and Welsh members of
the Westminster Parliament could debate and vote on English
matters such as education and health whereas English MPs
would have no involvement in such matters in Scotland or
Wales. If regional representation at Westminster were reduced,
as was the case when Northern Ireland had its own assembly
after partition, this would undermine any chance Labour might
have of achieving a working majority. Furthermore a Conservative
majority at Westminster and regional assemblies dominated by
Labour and Nationalists could provoke a constitutional crisis.

The most important question about the British electoral
system in general is the voting system to be used. Well before
the introduction of universal suffrage the system used in Britain,
variously termed simple plurality or first past the post was seen
as fundamentally unfair. The Proportional Representation
Society, later to become the Electoral Reform Society, was
founded in the 1880s, at the time of the third Reform Act: in
1910 a Royal Commission expressed support for a proportional system. A Speaker's Conference in 1917 supported the
Alternative Vote (not, of course, a proportional system), and in
the General Election of the following year Labour's result, 8%
of the seats from over 20% of the vote led Ramsay MacDonald
and others to concede that simple plurality was not necessarily
the most democratic. In 1930 Lloyd George offered to support
the Labour government for two or three years in return for
electoral reform, but although a bill to introduce the Alternative
Vote passed the Commons it was defeated by the House of
Lords.

Since 1945, if not before, support for reform of the voting
system has come mainly from third parties who naturally focus
on the argument that simple plurality distorts the wishes of the
voters by under-representing every party except the "big two".
Though this was most marked in 1983, as discussed in Chapter
9, it has been a feature of all post-war elections. The "unfair"

or "distortion" argument is not the only one, however. In the late 1970s and early 1980s many Conservatives were concerned that the system might produce a government even more unrepresentative than usual. In 1974 Labour had won an overall majority with less than 40% of the vote. If this was combined with a falling turnout, as seemed likely at the time, then it was possible that a Labour government could come to power with the support of barely 25% of the electorate but with a mandate for radical change such as full-scale nationalisation. Even as late as the 1983 General Election a majority of Conservatives asked were prepared to support electoral reform or at least consider it.

Subsequent General Elections made the prospect of any sort of Labour government look increasingly unlikely, and thoughts began to turn to electoral reform as the only means of breaking down the Conservative hegemony. The possibility seems to have been raised initially by Arthur Scargill, but it spread steadily through the Labour hierarchy during the 1980s, gaining particular force after the 1987 defeat. The Labour leadership was unimpressed, the most trenchant criticism of electoral reform coming from Roy Hattersley, who told the 1989 Party Conference, "I do not say that under PR we would never have a Labour government again, but I do say that we would never again have a Labour government that was able to carry out a Labour programme". Neil Kinnock also took this view: the Policy Review supported first past the post, and in the 1992 General Election manifesto the only commitment was "to encourage a wide and well-informed debate on the electoral system" with no indication that anything would necessarily be done about it. The main emphasis was on the possibility of electoral reform as a means of gaining the support of minority parties in the event of a hung parliament: in 1991 the Electoral Reform Society had found that 21% of Liberal voters would have switched to Labour in the event of a commitment to proportional representation.

As John Major pointed out during the 1992 campaign and others have pointed out since, electoral reform has usually been discussed in terms of party advantage, rather than the good of the political system as a whole, and certainly there has been little discussion of the different systems available and what changes each might cause. It is only possible to give a summary here, but fortunately two recent books cited in "Further Reading" (one by Andrew Reeve and Alan Ware, and the other edited for "Common Voice" by Gareth Smyth) discuss the practical and philosophical issues of electoral reform at the length the subject deserves.

A key problem with electoral reform is that there are several different systems in use in other countries, each of which would have different consequences if used in Britain. The simplest is a list system, where voters cast their vote for a party list either nationally or regionally, and seats are allocated according to the proportion of the vote gained. In countries such as Israel and the Netherlands, where the whole country is the constituency, the main drawback from the British point of view is the loss of the link between area and representative: representation becomes more proportional, less territorial. The Additional Member system used in Germany since the Second World War and likely to be adopted in Hungary and Bulgaria combines a list system with simple plurality. Voters have two votes, one for a constituency member, one for a party list, with members from the list being used to "top up" each party's representation to an equivalent of their vote share. The specific advantages are that the territorial basis of representation is partly retained, and party figures who lose their seats unexpectedly, such as Shirley Williams in 1979 and Chris Patten in 1992 can be put back through the party lists: there is no evidence that such MPs are seen as "second-class".

The other possibilities are "preferential" in that they involve voters putting candidates in order of preference rather than opting for a single candidate or party. The simpler is the Alternative Vote: here the requirement is for the winner to gain an overall majority. If no candidate reaches this point on the first count, the bottom candidate drops out, and his/her votes are reallocated according to second preference. In other words, voters are being asked "If you cannot have your first choice, who would you be prepared to put up with?" Under this system governments would have the support, albeit grudging, of a majority of the electorate, but third parties would be squeezed almost as badly. A variant of this system is the "Supplementary Vote" recommended by the Plant Commission in its final report: here voters register only first or second preferences, but otherwise the process is the same.

The most complex system, and the one favoured by pressure groups and third parties, is the Single Transferable Vote, used in Ireland even before partition. One significant difference from the systems described so far is that constituencies return several members. It is generally reckoned that there need to be at least five if the system is to work effectively, and when it was used to elect an assembly in Northern Ireland in 1973 the 12 Westminster constituencies were used, half returning six members, half seven to create an assembly of 78. This means that there are likely to be many candidates who have to be put in order of preference, and that a quota is needed to determine who has won a seat. Once a candidate achieves the quota his/her surplus votes are reallocated on second preference, removing the problem of "wasted" votes: if this still does not produce the number needed, bottom candidates drop out, as under the Alternative Vote system.

A great many advantages are claimed for this system. It is more or less proportional, like list systems, but preserves the links between members and areas. More important is its flexibility. The British system often requires voters to make a difficult choice: what should they do if they support a party but dislike the candidate, or vice versa? The opportunity to put all the candidates in order of preference removes this dilemma, and even enables voters to indicate the sort of coalition they would prefer if no party wins a majority. It is also claimed that minorities would be better represented under this system. Voters might be happier to include one woman or ethnic minority candidate among five or more when they might not "plump" for such a candidate as their sole representative. The disadvantages lie in the complexity of the process of voting. When this system was used in New York district elections in 1937 there were 99 candidates on a ballot paper four feet long. With constituencies returning at least five members there would be fifteen or more candidates to put in order of preference, and many voters would be tempted to "vote the ticket", in other words support all the candidates of one party, or to cast only one vote. Ireland has only 2.5 million voters: there is obviously no practical evidence as to how the Single Transferable Vote might work with much larger numbers. The process of finding a winner would certainly take much longer than at present if the Single Transferable Vote were to be used in Britain: even in Ireland the process can take up to a week.

Until 1992 there was little evidence as to how different voting systems might work in Britain, but work carried out at the London School of Economics following the 1992 General Election has provided some help (Table 19.1) Nationalist parties and the Green Party would do best under the Single Transferable Vote, and Labour would come nearest to the Conservatives under that system, but the Liberals would do better under the Additional Member System than any other, which is surprising in view of their long-term support for the STV. One thing at least is clear: that under the voting systems most favoured by advocates of reform, the Additional Member System and the Single Transferable Vote, no single party would come anywhere near an overall majority.

Table 19.1   *The 1992 General Election under alternative voting systems*

	Con.	Lab.	Lib.	Nat.	Green
Actual result	336	271	20	7	0
Alternative Vote	325	270	30	9	0
Additional Member System	268	232	116	18	0
Single Transferable Vote	256	250	102	20	6

Source: Dunleavy, Margetts and Weir, *Replaying the 1992 General Election*

One point of view claims that this would be a positive advantage, since both the dominance of one party for a lengthy period (for example the Conservatives from 1979) or the risk of violent change (as in the 1970s) have been harmful to progress. Any party with a majority can introduce any changes, no matter how drastic, and rely on a parliamentary majority to put them into law: when one party is almost certain to have a majority, significant constitutional change will not happen, because a government will not do anything which might reduce its power unless it has to. Where there are two parties alternating in government rights conferred by one government can be cancelled by the next. The need to work with other parties would restrain governments from partisan legislation which might be against the general interest. The likelihood of more frequent General Elections might help to concentrate the minds of governments: in Denmark they average an election every two years, and Ireland had five General Elections during the 1980s. Thus there would be an end to the erosion of citizens' rights since 1979 claimed by many civil liberties groups.

Supporters of electoral reform would argue that there is no need to say anything more, since the case for changing the system as a stage in full-scale constitutional reconstruction is self-evident. It is not as simple as that. In the first place, there is no such thing as a perfect voting system. It is not necessary to explore the highly theoretical approach put forward by Kenneth Arrow in 1951 and discussed by Reeve and Ware to realise that no system can hope to satisfy all the criteria, and that solving one problem may create another which is at least as bad. Thus in Britain the Single Transferable Vote is more flexible and arguably represents voters' wishes more accurately than simple plurality, but is more complex for the voters and slower in producing a result, not only in respect of the seats gained by the various parties, but also in the formation of a government.

This is probably the most important issue in considering the question of changing our voting system: as Reeve and Ware point out, one reason for the persistence of a system is uncertainty as to the consequences of change. If no party could form a government on its own, it would either try to govern as a minority, as Labour did in 1974, or to reach a deal with one or more other parties, as Labour did informally in 1924 and after losing their majority in 1976. In the past coalitions have only happened under stress, as in 1915 or 1931, and have involved acrimony in their setting up or their collapse (as in 1945). The disputes between the parties, Labour and Liberals, Labour and Ulster Unionists over the Maastricht debate and whether opposition parties ought to support the government or try to bring it down provided little encouragement that they might be able to work together in government. On the other hand such agreements have become increasingly common in local government. Deals were struck between the parties in the run-up to the 1989 county council elections involving electoral pacts (parties standing down in seats they could not win, a sort of organised tactical voting) and after May 1991 there were more hung local councils than were under Conservative or Labour control, a situation worsened from the Conservative point of view in May 1993. In such counties as Kent the parties have reached some sort of agreement on sharing responsibility, however shakily. Many Liberal or SDP councillors pointed out at the time of the merger that they were already merged at local level, so why not nationally? We could even see local democracy determining the national pattern, rather than the other way round.

The question of deals between parties raises an important constitutional issue largely overlooked by supporters of electoral reform. Many of the systems proposed involve greatly increased power for party managers: for example in a list system loyalists can be put at the top, nuisances at the bottom of a party list. The claim that the Single Transferable Vote enables voters to show the sort of coalition they want is very unlikely to be borne out in practice. Coalitions happen as a result of concessions by at least one of the parties involved, which implies discussions between leaders and managers which may have nothing to do with preferences expressed by voters. For example the combined vote of Labour and Liberals has exceeded that of the Conservatives in every election since 1959, but it is difficult to believe that a Labour/Liberal coalition was always what the voters wanted.

All this runs the risk of distancing voters from the outcome of the election, and thus producing apathy or hostility. In the spring of 1993 a substantial majority in Italy voted to replace their proportional voting system (a modified list system) by simple plurality because it was blamed for widespread corruption and inefficiency, as well as the hectic series of changes of government, averaging more than one a year since the Second World War. Admittedly many of Italy's political problems and the fragmentation of their political system have roots deep in history, but the decision ran counter to the trend in Eastern Europe, where none of the newly-independent states of the Soviet bloc opted for simple plurality. If Italy has become a byword for the inefficiency of proportional systems, Germany has been claimed as a vindication. Yet even here, the voting system has been blamed for a political system which has become stagnant rather than stable, and thus unable to cope with the strain of reunification. Some politicians have apparently adopted the policy of the Vicar of Bray, of remaining in power whatever the government may be.

Britain's electoral system rests on assumptions going back nearly a century. The danger is that it will become part of the "heritage", kept in being through nostalgia or because the forces which could change it would be harmed by any possible change. Britain has never had the sort of violent disruption which has required a total re-examination of electoral and political processes, nor has any party seriously examined electoral reform as a means of gaining or keeping power. Until one of these situations applies, General Elections tomorrow will differ from elections yesterday and today in detail, not in substance.

Further reading

Les Back and John Solomos, *Who Represents Us?*, Research Paper 3 (London, Birkbeck College), 1992

Shaun Bowler and David Farrell (eds), *Electoral Strategies and Political Marketing* (London, Macmillan), 1992

George Brown, *In My Way* (London, Gollancz), 1971

David E. Butler, *The British Electoral System since 1918* (Oxford University Press), 1986

British General Elections since 1945 (Oxford, Basil Blackwell), 1989

B. Jones and L. Robins (eds), *Two Decades in British Politics* (Manchester University Press), 1992; see chapter on "Voting Behaviour and the Party System"

David E. Butler and Dennis Kavanagh, *The British General Election of February 1974* (London, Macmillan), 1974

The British General Election of October 1974 (London, Macmillan), 1975

The British General Election of 1979 (London, Macmillan), 1980

The British General Election of 1983 (London, Macmillan), 1984

The British General Election of 1987 (London, Macmillan), 1988

The British General Election of 1992 (London, Macmillan), 1993

David E. Butler and Anthony King,

The British General Election of 1964 (London, Macmillan), 1965

The British General Election of 1966 (London, Macmillan), 1967

David E. Butler and Michael Pinto-Duschinsky, *The British General Election of 1970* (London, Macmillan), 1971

James Callaghan, *Time and Chance* (London, Collins), 1987

David Childs, *Britain since 1945*, 3rd edition (London: Routledge), 1992

Frank Conley, *The 1992 General Election: The End of Psephology?* (*Talking Politics*, Summer 1993)

Patrick Cosgrave, *The Lives of Enoch Powell* (London, The Bodley Head), 1989

Richard Crossman, *The Crossman Diaries*, ed. Anthony Howard (London, Mandarin), 1991

David Denver, *Elections and Voting Behaviour in Britain* (Oxford: Philip Allan), 1990

The 1992 General Election: In Defence of Psephology (*Talking Politics*, Autumn 1992)

David Denver and Gordon Hands (eds) *Issues and Controversies in British Electoral Behaviour* (Hemel Hempstead, Harvester Wheatsheaf), 1992

Patrick Dunleavy, Helen Margetts and Stuart Weir, *Replaying the 1992 General Election*, LSE Public Policy Paper 3 (London School of Economics), 1992

Martin Gilbert, *Churchill: A Life* (London, Heinemann), 1991

Kenneth Harris, *Attlee* (London, Weidenfeld and Nicholson), 1982

Anthony Heath, Roger Jowell and John Curtice, *How Britain Votes* (Oxford, Pergamon Press), 1985

Hilde T. Himmelweit, Patrick Humphries and Marianne Jaeger, *How Voters Decide* (Milton Keynes, Open University Press), 1985

Alistair Horne, *Macmillan: (i) 1894–1956; (ii) 1957–1986* (London, Macmillan), 1988

Robert Rhodes James, *Anthony Eden* (London, Macmillan), 1986

Bill Jones and Dennis Kavanagh, (eds) *British Politics Today, 4th edition* (Manchester University Press), 1990

Brian Lapping, *The Labour Government 1964–1970* (Harmondsworth, Penguin), 1970

Ken Livingstone, *If Voting Changed Anything, They'd Abolish It* (London, Collins), 1987

Austen Morgan, *J. Ramsay MacDonald* (Manchester University Press), 1987

Pippa Norris, *The 1987 General Election: the Hidden Agenda* (*Teaching Politics*, September 1987)

Edward Pearce, *Election Rides* (London, Faber and Faber), 1992

Ben Pimlott, *Harold Wilson* (London, Harper Collins), 1992

Clive Ponting, *Breach of Promise* (London, Hamish Hamilton), 1989

Andrew Reeve and Alan Ware *Electoral Systems* (London, Routledge), 1992

Nicholas Ridley, *My Style of Government: The Thatcher Years* (London, Hutchinson), 1991

Lynton Robins (ed.), *Political Institutions in Britain: Development and Change* (Harlow, Longman), 1987

Shamit Saggar, *Race and Politics in Britain* (Hemel Hempstead, Harvester Wheatsheaf), 1992

Martin J. Smith and Joanna Spear (eds), *The Changing Labour Party* (London: Routledge), 1992

Gareth Smyth (ed.), *Refreshing the Parts* (London, Lawrence and Wishart), 1992

Rodney Tyler, *Campaign: The Selling of the Prime Minister* (London, Grafton Books), 1987

Des Wilson, *Battle for Power* (London, Sphere Books), 1987

Harold Wilson, *Final Term* (London, Weidenfeld/Joseph), 1979

Hugo Young, *One of Us*, final edition (London, Macmillan), 1991

Index